# HOW

## To Beat

# DEPRESSION

## with the

# BIBLE

Taylor Johnson

ISBN 979-8-88616-967-6 (paperback)
ISBN 979-8-88616-968-3 (digital)



Christian Faith Publishing
832 Park Avenue
Meadville, PA 16335
www.christianfaithpublishing.com

Printed in the United States of America

*I pray that God, the source of hope, will fill you completely with joy and peace because you trust in him. Then you will overflow with confident hope through the power of the Holy Spirit.*

—Romans 15:13 (NLT)

# PROLOGUE

Living in a generation where the most overdiagnosed ailment is depression can be troubling in multiple ways, the first of which is the overprescribed medication list for this illness. Every medication prescribed for depression has a possible side effect of worsening the depression and/or causing suicidal thoughts or actions. Does that seem like it's worth trying? For millions of people, it is. In the United States alone, as of 2018, there were a reported 42.25 million people on antidepressants. They were willing to risk getting worse so that they could have a slight chance to feel a little bit better. In this book, I will share the best and most effective way to beat depression: with the Bible.

Depression is not something that's new; on the contrary, depression has existed for thousands of years. In the majority of cases of suicide, it was due to depression. Some cultures, like ancient Japanese societies, have viewed suicide as the only honorable action that you can take after failing. Nonetheless, the vast majority of the time, it's from depression that people will turn to suicide, drug/alcohol abuse, self-mutilation, or even getting into specific lines of work.

So what is depression? Depression is best described as being the lack of love for life. Think about it: is there something as tragic as waking up every morning only to wish you could go back to sleep, not because you're tired but simply because you don't want to live your life? If the first word out of your mouth when you wake up has four letters, there is a chance you understand what I'm talking about when I say this.

Depression comes and goes for some; for others, it's like the annoying in-laws that you wish would leave already, but guess what, they are moving in.

Everything in this book comes from my own experience with depression. For literally as long as I can remember, I've battled with depression. As a child, I couldn't explain what I felt, so I lashed out in many different ways. My mom called them the three C's. She'd tell me that all I do is *criticize*, *condemn*, and *complain*. She wasn't wrong. I was a negative kid, expressing my dislike of the world without knowing why. She would tell me that I had a bad attitude all the time. Again, she wasn't wrong.

When I was nine years old, I remember trying to figure out how I could kill myself. I wish more than anything that I was making that up… I'm not. It wasn't like a one-time thing; it was a persistent thought where I'd constantly imagine the items around me and try to figure out how I could use them to end my life.

"If I jumped off that…if I ran in front of that car…if I stabbed myself with that…where should I stab myself? How far do I need to fall? How fast does the car have to move? What if I drank that? What if I hold my breath for a long time? What if I choke myself? What if…what if…what if…"

I vividly remember these thoughts as a child; they went on for some time. When I was fourteen, I got some excellent advice: fake it 'til you make it. I was told to act happy, act like everything is okay, and then somehow it will be eventually. I mean that sincerely, that wasn't sarcastic; it was genuinely excellent advice. When I started to pretend to be happy, people around me got happier. People smiled more. I wasn't getting yelled at for being negative; surprisingly, it made my life a little better but only a little bit.

Being raised in a Christian home was a tremendous blessing, but at the same time, it was tricky. It was tricky because as a kid, you were taught that God is real, just like Santa, the Easter Bunny, and the Tooth Fairy. So once you get to the age when you figure out that holiday figures are fake, it makes you start to doubt if God is real. That tends to make life suck quite a bit more than it already did. I spent my days and nights pondering over that question: is God real? If Santa is fake, why would God be real? To be clear, this is in no way saying not to raise kids Christian but maybe to peek deeper into teaching them about fictitious characters that stem from pagan religions (i.e., Santa is actually based on a Nordic god called Oden) so that they don't end up correlating God with Santa like millions of people, including myself, have done.

This confusion over reality was the event that first planted doubt in my mind. When I was thirteen, however, I met a girl that would later become my first girlfriend. You know, the first love crap that destroys every mind. When I was fifteen, this girl and I started dating. Months passed before I was head over heels, madly in love with this girl. She was in every thought I had; she was the first thing I thought of when I woke up and the last thing I thought of when I went to sleep.

With her, life felt real…it felt like it mattered. I felt like I mattered. She was the break in my life from the monotonous day-to-day repetitions of disappointment and resentment. I trusted her with my life, with my heart, with my soul…until one day she ended things. I didn't know why, and she just said she wasn't happy anymore. This happened right before Christmas, not long after I turned sixteen. That was my first sleepless night. I developed a horrible case of insomnia and a night terror disorder. To this day, I still suffer from insomnia. I, however, refused to take any form of sleeping medication, knowing that the body would eventually fix itself. Though insomnia still lingers in my life, hiding behind corners and under beds, I have gotten significantly better. I was at the point of getting, maybe, two to four hours of sleep a night if I was lucky.

As time progressed, that turned to four to six hours, and now, I occasionally get eight hours of sleep again. It's rare, but it's progress. To make things worse, not long after all of this occurred, I found out why she left me, or rather who she left me for. I asked her multiple times if there was someone else, and she said, "No, I just need to work on myself for a while."

I believed her until I caught her in that lie. That's the issue with still seeing people that you break up with on a regular basis—you'll see them move on and, in my case, you'll catch them in a lie. From there, I found out that she had been lying to me about a few different things, about which I won't bore you with the details. The day that I caught her in the lie, that's when life went from bad to worse.

I believed every single word that came out of her mouth. Why would she lie? She loved me, didn't she? Man, I was stupid. Anyway, I connected it in my head, that if what she told me wasn't real, then nothing was. God can't be real; anything my parents told me: all lies. Even my own existence, I started to think it was a lie. That's what extreme sleep deprivation does to a teenage mind. I hated my life, not just that I wasn't happy; I *hated* my life and I really didn't have a reason to. Getting an average of two to four hours of sleep every night (as I mentioned), having the exact same nightmare every single night, I wanted to die so bad. The only comfort I found was in the images my mind would summon of me no longer breathing. This wasn't because my life was actually bad; it was all in my head and the way my mind perceived the world around me.

I contemplated suicide every single day for about a year and a half. I never attempted it. At the time, I was learning a lot about anatomy to understand a severe injury that I had recently experienced, so I knew exactly how to do the deed without a risk of failure. The injury was debilitating and made matters worse. I had torn ligaments in both of my shoulders and got my entire spine twisted, so every muscle in the right side of my back went into spasm. The pain was so terrible I could barely move for three days. Add this pain to my mental state and lack of sleep. Looking back, I'm surprised I'm still here. Only God is to thank for that.

It wasn't until about a year after my breakup that I began to see a pattern with numbers. It was bizarre. I started seeing the numbers 118 and 9. For example, that first girlfriend, I began doing jiujitsu on January 18th, 2009 (1-18-09). There I met a friend and his older *sister*...yep. Her birthday was ironically January 18th...1-18. Looking at clocks, I'd always look at 11:08, 11:18, 1:18, or 8:11, and it would just catch my eye every time. There was a rapper I liked whose name was associated with the number 9; his birthday was November 8th (11-8).

Years pass, and I was driving to work; I was dating a girl that worked with me at a haunted house. On my way to the job and to see her, I was driving on a road with three lanes. I was in the middle of the three, and there were three cars side by side one another in front of me in these three lanes. All three vehicles had license plates that ended with 118. When I got to work, she broke up with me. I used to have a list of over one thousand occurrences of this number correlated to something significant or impactful in my life, and it freaked me out. I started to think that it was too coincidental to be random. I started looking and I couldn't find any significance in that number at all. Then one day, randomly scrolling through social media, I saw a Bible verse about trust. "It is better to take refuge in the Lord than to trust in humans." This verse is Psalm 118:8 (NIV). Reading that literally knocked me back. I saw the number, and it was so close to 1189. So immediately, I went into the Bible and I read Psalm 118. There were nine verses in that passage that made me cry and feel this immediate relief as if a massive boulder had been lifted off me. It was Psalm 118:5–14, which (in the NIV) reads:

> When hard pressed, I cried to the Lord; he brought me into a spacious place. The Lord is with me; I will not be afraid. What can mere mortals do to me? The Lord is with me; he is my helper. I look in triumph on my enemies. It is better to take refuge in the Lord than to trust in humans. It is better to take refuge in the Lord than to trust in princes. All the nations surrounded me, but in the name of the Lord I cut them down. They surrounded me on every side, but in the name of the Lord I cut them down. They swarmed around me like bees, but they were consumed as quickly as burning thorns; in the name of the Lord I cut them down. I was pushed back and about to fall, but the Lord helped me. The Lord is my strength and my defense; he has become my salvation.

These verses, these nine verses from Psalm 118, saved my life. I started reading the Bible obsessively, looking at every account of 118. Starting at the beginning, I started looking at Genesis 1:18, Genesis 8:11, Genesis 11:8, and so on. During my research, I found out that there are precisely 1,189 chapters in the Bible. I found out that if you went chapter by chapter to the center of the Bible, you'd arrive at Psalm 118. If you went verse by verse to the very center of the Bible, you'd find Psalm 118:8. There was absolutely no way that was a coincidence.

So now you know the beginning of this, now let me walk you through what I found. Reading this book isn't going to fix your depression. However, if you apply the lessons that I'll teach, you will be able to beat your depression.

Before you read this, I want to make this as straightforward as possible: sincerely putting your trust in Christ alone is the key to beating depression and being saved. However, *putting trust in Christ does not mean you will never be depressed.* I want to explain this very clearly so that there is no confusion on what I am saying. There is something called a prosperity gospel; this is a blatant lie taught by morally corrupt televangelists who are selling lies to people, masquerading it as Christianity. This book is not that.

The whole "believe in Jesus and life will be awesome" lie is one of the most dangerous ideologies surrounding modern Christianity. I am in no way saying that you will suddenly be happy and wealthy with no issues or stress in your life ever again. Rather, it's just the opposite. Jesus told us that the world would hate us for loving Him *(John 15:18).*

He promised that we would face trials, tribulation, and persecution for following Him. In fact, many of His followers became martyrs for Christ. Some were beheaded, stabbed to death, thrown off buildings, or even crucified themselves. Not one of them ever denounced their faith in Jesus throughout the torture and excruciating deaths they faced. The reason why is as plain as these words are written, they saw Jesus do impossible acts: heal people by touching them, cast out demons by speaking, make the blind see, make the deaf hear, walk on water, die the death that he predicted, and come back from the dead. For us, it is a belief in Jesus, a trust that is based on faith. It was an indisputable, irrefutable fact for the disciples (the firsthand witnesses to Jesus's ministry).

If someone is making it up, as skeptics would claim the disciples did, not one single person would ever be willing to be, for example, crucified upside down after being brutally whipped and beaten as Peter was, unless they were completely and totally insane, which are the only options for Jesus, actually. Either He was the most insane human who has ever lived, who somehow predicted the future flawlessly on countless occasions, performed miracles, and was resurrected from the dead by some mysterious freak accident…or He is God.

So by beating depression, what do I mean? How is this going to help you? What is beating depression? Well, as we see throughout the world, the end result of depression is often suicide. In other cases, people who are depressed turn to alcohol or drug abuse, or they hurt other people, lashing out in abusive and violent ways. To beat depression simply means that you don't let it win, you don't take your own life, you don't turn to addictions, you don't hurt anyone—that is beating depression.

As with any debate or presentation of information, it is important to set firm definitions for what shall be discussed. Primarily, the term *depression* must be defined so there is a clear understanding between us (you, the reader, and myself) on what is being articulated. Firstly, what is depression? Depression in our context will be characterized, as previously mentioned, as a disdain for or disliking of life itself. Depression is like waking up in the morning with the feeling of having hundreds of pounds of rocks stacked on top of you. You know the rocks aren't there, but they might as well be; you can't get out of bed regardless of their existence. Depression is like living in a perpetual funeral service; everything seems sad and disappointing. Some who have been depressed have equated it to living in a gray world, void of color, absent of excitement, lacking joy, missing that which fuels life: hope.

Think of the most significant disappointment that you've ever faced. Think back to exactly how you felt the moment you realized that what you had hoped for would not become a reality. That promotion at work. The marriage proposal to your now ex-girlfriend. When you discovered your dad was never coming home. A time that you felt utterly defeated by life. Think back to the way you felt at that very moment. Imagine that feeling being forcefully draped over your body from the second you wake up to the second you fall asleep every single day. That is depression. With the night terrors that I was experiencing, I felt that feeling every second of every day and every night.

Depression can come alone or as a side effect of something else. For example, bipolar, schizophrenic, and manic people (to name a few types of personality disorders) will suffer from depression as a side effect of their domineering mental illness. While the steps in this book may help those people, I cannot say so with any certainty. The depression I faced was alone and not a side effect of another ailment. I used to have severe anxiety as a side effect of depression; it has gone away significantly due to beating depression. To be clear, people who are depressed without an underlying mental illness are the people who will have the best luck at beating depression by following the steps in this book.

Why are people depressed? Well, look at life. Life is full of death, and therefore, some can't see the purpose of pushing through the constant monotony of life if the end is inevitable and bleak. As mentioned previously, the purpose of this book is to help you beat depression, not to get rid of it. So the best way to beat depression is to establish a love and appreciation for life. It, therefore, could be argued that we are depressed because of death and a lack of purpose.

It could also be argued that we are depressed due to feelings of inadequacy in various stages of life. For men, you may feel that you're not enough of a man. I know this may not sound like much, but it can be devastating in that men cannot be men in today's society. The constant berating of masculinity and the excessive claims that being manly is somehow toxic or even unnatural is a horrible lie. From a young age, men in our culture are being beaten with ideas of what they should be instead of letting them be themselves. Men aren't supposed to be told that aggression is destructive. Men aren't supposed to be told violence is never okay.

These are lies that lead to weak men. Weak men who lack true masculinity lack the ability to be emotionally available. It's weak, emasculated men who abuse their wives and children or hurt others. As the Warrior Poet, John Lovell, states: "We should be lions and lambs, lovers and fighters, warriors and poets, and I think if you're not a good lover, you're deficient as a fighter."

This is true masculinity, but we have been taught that it's something to be ashamed of or avoided. Real men need to be caring, loving, dangerous protectors who can go from reading a bedtime story to his kids and then immediately be able to flip the switch and be unbelievably violent at a moment's notice. That is what this world needs: good men who are willing to do very violent things to evil people to protect the innocent. So, men, as you're reading this, think about what has depressed you. Is it someone trying to make you feel weak? Are you weak? Let's diagnose your mindset and see how we can fix it.

For women, it's a very similar form of inadequacy. From that young age, girls are taught that there is only one acceptable outcome in their life, and if they don't achieve it, they aren't a woman. They are taught conflicting singular outcomes that confuse them until the damage leaves its impression deeper than it was thought possible. Social pressures are being forced, and a woman can never really think about what she wants for her own life because of these pressures weighing down on her. You may want a traditional family life, but you're being told that it's giving in to the patriarchy. You may want to have a career and be told you're not supposed to do that because you must have kids. All of this is damaging but not nearly as harmful as the beauty industry.

If you're looking for a body positivity book that will tell you what you want to hear about obesity, this isn't it. I care too much about my readers' physical and mental health to perpetuate a lie that being obese is healthy or even attractive (men and women alike). That being said, what standard are you holding yourself to? What is your body type? What is your height? What is your structural build? Are you in a healthy range when it comes to your BMI (body mass index)? These things matter so you can start looking at yourself realistically instead of comparing yourself to women in magazines.

If you are five feet tall and want to look like a six-foot-tall model with professional trainers, dieticians, makeup artists, and designers who are tailoring the outfits to fit her perfectly, wake up and stop comparing yourself to fiction. This is what society wants. This is what these businesses want. They want you to feel insecure and awful about yourself so that they can sell you diet pills and makeup that will make you think you're prettier so men will love you. I hate to be the one who breaks this news to you, ladies, but men don't care about looks nearly as much as you think they do. Seriously.

When a single man walks into a room, he will scan every woman in there to see if he has a chance with them. The one he will talk to isn't the prettiest. The one he talks to is the one that he feels is the safest. Men don't want to be rejected, so they avoid it at all costs. This rejection emasculates them and makes them feel like failures as a man. However, sometimes they risk it because they want to pursue you just as bad as you want them to.

My point with this is simple: if you take hours to get dressed, do your makeup, style your hair perfectly to attract a man when you go out while your friend goes out with minimal effort put in, chances are, your friend will be talked to more. Is it because you're not as attractive? Not at all. You got noticed more than her, but she's more approachable than you. She appears to be more laid-back and probably more friendly. Men like to hunt; they don't like to miss. So stop holding yourself to a high standard of beauty and perfection. If a guy only cares about your looks, he's a weak man, and you should avoid him, anyway. Men, the same applies to you; avoid superficial women who only care about looks. These traits are very temporary and are mostly useless. Attraction is necessary but not nearly as important as sharing morals and goals.

Females, in general, tend to care more about looks than men. There are always exceptions, but generally, this is the case across all walks of life. Look at animals, for example. A male mallard duck has a beautiful green head, purple hues in his feathers, a bright beak, and patterns under his wings. A female duck is gray and brown. The male must be beautiful for the female to notice him. The male isn't caring as much about the appearance of the female. This also applies to many other animals, even down to fish.

From my personal experience and those I've questioned on the subject, the main thing men look for in a woman is her ability to put in effort. What do I mean by this? Well, I'm not talking about the effort put into getting dressed to the nines. I'm talking about the initial meeting. Many women will try to play "hard to get" or will be standoffish because they want the guy to try harder. Meet him half-way and show interest back; that is far more effective than spending hundreds of dollars on makeup and uncomfortable shoes.

Why is this the most desired trait? When a woman tries in the beginning, it's taken as a sign that she will try in the future. Relationships are roller coasters with rapid inclines and declines that make a lot of people sick. When only one-half of the relationship tries, the appeal of getting off the ride grows immensely. This goes both ways in the relationship. Of course, all I'm expressing is the best trait to work on in the beginning of a relationship instead of being told how to look.

Now the sensitive subject, weight. The reason why being overweight is not attractive (if you actually think it is, you're a rarity or simply don't care about it) is because of what it says about you. Obesity is associated with being lazy, self-hatred, and poor decision-making. This is why it's not attractive. Your outward appearance is a reflection of your inner personality. This is for both men and women! Don't think I'm directing this at women only! If you don't take care of yourself and don't love yourself, it turns away people who are looking for love.

Why did I go on this little tangent? Inadequacy. The primary stem that inadequacy grows from is the opinions of you that are held by others. It's your failures, your appearance, how masculine/feminine you are. It is all impactful in your mind and alters your outlook on life. Stop caring about the opinions of others and live your life the way you want to live it. Ultimately, life is individual, and you need to make choices for yourself; don't let others choose your life.

Trauma, rejection, inadequacy, death…these can all together or individually cause depression to grow like a toxic weed whose roots strangle the life out of all the flowers in the garden. These things can make life seem hard. Life is hard, and it comes to an end. We all just inevitably die, so is it worth it to keep playing the game? It depends on what happens after we die. Why are we here? What's the purpose of life? Why do we die? All of these questions and more will be covered and answered in the following steps.

As I mentioned, I used to contemplate suicide on a regular basis; this isn't the case anymore. I still have crappy days. I still feel sad and depressed, mad and upset. I still occasionally find myself worrying about how others see me when I know it doesn't matter what they think. Overall, though, I beat depression because of the steps in this book. The steps in this book are based on the Bible as its primary source. Aside from that, there will also be personal realizations that I have made, as well as lessons based on psychology, sociology, philosophy, and logic that I will use to teach you how I beat depression with the Bible. Take these steps to heart and test them out. I pray that you find success as I have. Enjoy!

# STEP 1

# Find the Source

While every person is different, everyone shares a common origin story. We had something happen to us that triggered the most substantial surge of depression. So what caused yours? For me, it was trust being broken. For you, it could have been the loss of a loved one, abuse suffered, stress, neglect, insomnia—there's a number of potential causes or accelerants for depression. The goal now is to find the source of your depression's fire and extinguish it. Following this metaphor, depression is truly like a fire: the longer it burns, the hotter it gets; the hotter it gets, the more intensely it spreads.

What brought me comfort in the initial nine verses I read was the assurance that God is listening. He answers prayers. He is trustworthy. This is something that is constantly repeated in the Bible.

> So do not fear, for I am with you; do not be
> dismayed, for I am your God. I will strengthen
> you and help you; I will uphold you with my
> righteous right hand. *(Isaiah 41:10 NIV)*

> Trust in the Lord with all your heart and
> lean not on your own understanding; in all your
> ways submit to him, and he will make your paths
> straight. *(Proverbs 3:5-6 NIV)*

> This is the confidence we have in approach-
> ing God: that if we ask anything according to his
> will, he hears us. And if we know that he hears
> us—whatever we ask—we know that we have
> what we asked of him. *(1 John 5:14-15 NIV)*

This step is the first and most crucial step because we need to be able to forgive. A lot of people confuse forgiving and forgetting, so let me briefly explain the difference. We need to remember the root of what caused the issue but not hold a grudge against the person or persons who contributed to it. Even in the case of death, some people will hold hostile feelings toward the one who has passed with subconscious feelings of disdain toward the person who "left" us. They feel abandoned by the loss. That abandonment can lead to resentment, depression, and a loss of a motivational drive to succeed in life.

Suppose the trigger of your depression came from something a lot more intimate, like a betrayal or a situation of abuse. In that case, this can be harder to forgive. Whether it be a physically, mentally, or sexually abusive situation from a spouse, sibling, family member, friend, or even a stranger, we must learn a lesson from the situation and yet be able to forgive that person for their crimes against us. If we put the blame on someone else for our own unhappiness, we can never actually overcome or beat our depression. Though someone may have caused it, we don't have to associate that person with the trauma. In other words, we aren't responsible for the actions of others, but we are exclusively liable for our reactions.

It could have been a terrible event. However, no matter how awful or depraved the visceral act was, our response to that event is going to be what determines our future. We must be able to hold ourselves up and pull ourselves through the hardship. In learning the foundation of our pain, we must also learn a way to transfer the blame from the party responsible onto the person who is dealing with it—you. I'm not saying to blame yourself for the issues that you've lived through; I'm saying that you need to take responsibility for your own current mental state.

> Be kind and compassionate to one another, forgiving each other, just as in Christ God forgave you. *(Ephesians 4:32 NIV)*

> For if you forgive other people when they sin against you, your heavenly Father will also forgive you. *(Matthew 6:14 NIV)*

So why is this the first step? Why will this be the most crucial starting point on our journey to recovering from the haunting, persistent depression that makes life bleak and empty? Well, just as Jesus forgives us, we must forgive others. As you'll find in the following steps, the goal with this book isn't going to be eliminating depression; it's to strive to act more like Jesus and live in His example. From there, true joy, happiness, and a newfound hope in life will be discovered as your depression slips away from existence. The biblical definition of being holy is to be like Christ. This is physically impossible for us. However, we must strive for that perfection in order to defeat depression and find joy

> Do not judge, and you will not be judged. Do not condemn, and you will not be condemned. Forgive, and you will be forgiven. *(Luke 6:37 NIV)*

If we strive to live like Jesus and make that our primary goal, the effects will come naturally. So to repeat, step 1: find the initial cause of your depression and forgive it.

Forgiving someone for hurting you doesn't make it okay that they did something to you. Forgiving isn't permitting. If you were abused, you aren't telling that person what they did is okay. You are releasing them of the hostility, hatred, and resentment that you feel for them. You are freeing your own mind of the enmity and hatred you hold toward that person. You no longer have harsh feelings toward the person that wronged you; therefore, you're no longer keeping their face in the front of your mind. So how do you forgive someone for hurting you if that someone is you?

What I mean by this is that we are constantly haunted by the memories of the mistakes we have made in our lives that led us to add them to our list of regrets. We remember the regretful decisions so much clearer than we can remember the moments that would make our future selves proud. What is it that you did that is haunting you with this perpetual guilt? Did you hurt someone? Did you cheat? Did you lie to someone you loved? Did you have regrettable last words to someone who passed? Did you do drugs at a young age without realizing that the long-term effects on your body and brain would later start to surface? Did you have kids when you were young? What is it that you hold against yourself?

Most people have many regrets that haunt them. For some, it will be the marriage they should never have rushed into. For others, it will be trusting someone they knew wasn't worthy of trust. For others still, it will be a pang of guilt that they never lived up to their goals. The easiest way to forgive someone or even yourself is to change your perspective on the events that played out.

Think about the positives of the situation (depending on the specific case, this could be very hard to do). What did you learn from the situation? Did *anyone* benefit from it? Whatever it is that happened, you can change your outlook on it by accepting the objective reality of the past. As I mentioned before, some think they've had kids too young, as an example. This is a horrible mindset. View it differently. You didn't have kids too early; God's plans happened exactly as they should have.

There was a girl that I used to know. She had a horrific childhood at the hands of her stepdad. At the age of ten, she began using heroin. At the age of twelve, she was utterly addicted to it as well as many other drugs. She once told me that the only drug she never tried was shrooms. At the age of fourteen, she was taken to the hospital for an overdose on heroin. It was then that she found out she was pregnant. Having a value for human life, she didn't even consider the murder of that child to be an option, as many do. Instead, she got clean.

The withdrawals from something like heroin will make you wish for death. Weeks of agonizing pain, vomiting, diarrhea, fever, sweating, chills, aches, and constant discomfort—she went through all of that for the baby's health. I bring up this story because God saved her life with that baby. She had that baby right before she turned fifteen years old. She has been clean since she got that news.

When I first learned this story, it was before I met her child. I immediately thought about how the baby's development could have been affected. I was expecting this kid to be mentally slow and possibly have some physical deformities. I met her daughter on her fifth birthday when I took her and her mom to a hibachi-style restaurant to celebrate. That's when I noticed that this kid wasn't deformed in any way. She wasn't disabled and she wasn't slow; she was perfect. To this day, that was the smartest kid I have ever met.

Her mom wasn't religious and never talked to her daughter about God or anything of that nature. So you can imagine my surprise when we were driving one day and this little girl randomly asked, "What's a soul?"

I was dumbfounded. I was amazed at the overly complex question I got from this little girl. The next question brought a literal tear to my eye: "Who is God?"

The point of me explaining this is to show you that sometimes, that which is scary, inconvenient, and uncomfortable could be a blessing from God disguised as a curse or a burden—at least from our perspective. If this woman didn't get pregnant at the age of fourteen, I have no doubt she would have died before she turned eighteen as some of her friends did. She probably thought she was having a baby too early. Fortunately, God's plan worked out better than hers.

Everything that may seem negative at the time is for a particular reason. I'm not sure what the reason is for the vast majority of seemingly negative occurrences. Hindsight is 20/20 only for human reasoning; it can be tough or impossible to find God's purpose in what happens. In the example I've provided, we can see only part of God's purpose (saving her life). So why did God save her life? That woman now has other kids as well; maybe part of the purpose was so her other kids could come into this world. Perhaps one of her kids or even one of her grandkids will grow up to do something extraordinary. God sees and knows all, but we sure can't.

For something as extreme as WWII, we can even see not positives but reasons why it had to happen. The Bible predicted the rebirth of Israel; that rebirth happened immediately after WWII's ending as a direct result of the Holocaust. The Bible talked about how the Jewish people would come from all corners of the earth to return to their homeland; it happened immediately after that rebirth *(Ezekiel 20)*.

It's essential to try to find the reason for what happened to you. However, it is not necessary to find this reason in order to forgive. It will definitely help you to forgive, but don't focus on this. If God wants you to see the reason, you'll see it. It may take weeks, months, years, decades, or even generations to unearth the purpose for something.

In Genesis 38, there is a man named Judah. Judah is supposed to wed his son, Er, to a woman named Tamar, and so he does. God sees that Er is evil (for an untold reason), and God kills Er. So his brother Onan comes into play. In accordance with the law of Moses, Onan was to have a child with Tamar on his brother's behalf and raise the child for his brother. Onan refuses to do this and pulls out to ejaculate when having sex with Tamar so that he wouldn't have what would be considered his brother's son. God killed Onan for this evilness.

You might be thinking, *That doesn't seem right.* Did he get killed by God for pulling out? Technically yes but also no. Just remember this, we will hit back on why he was killed. Anyway, Judah tells Tamar to live with her father as a widow until Judah's third son, Shela, is old enough for marriage. Time passes, Judah forgets. Judah's wife dies, Shela grows up, Tamar gets impatient. She goes out, covering her face with a veil, to speak with Judah. Seeing the location that she was in and not being able to see her face, Judah thinks she is a prostitute. He's lonely and asks her to have sex with him. She plays along and sleeps with him.

Judah says he can't pay her yet, so he gives her his seal and his staff as collateral. Time passes, and Judah hears that his daughter-in-law, Tamar, has whored herself out. He gets furious and goes out to find her so she can be stoned. Upon seeing her, she presents his staff and seal. He realizes that he was in the wrong and was being a hypocrite. She got pregnant by Judah during the whole prostitute debacle.

Now you might be thinking, *Why is* any *of this relevant?* Well, if we read in Matthew 1, it lists the lineage and ancestry of Jesus. In order for Jesus to have been born through the lineage over one thousand years later, Tamar had to have a baby, Perez, for Christ to come down the bloodline as God promised. This is also why it was evil that Onan refused to impregnate Tamar. It wasn't because he ejaculated on the ground; it's because he was refusing to fulfill the law of Moses, in which case meant he was preventing the lineage that led to Jesus. That's why he was killed by God, not because he got semen on the dirt. This passage is often used to reference why masturbation or birth control is wrong by people who do not understand the biblical context. I'm not saying whether or not masturbation or birth control is sinful. I'm saying this passage is not about that. Those ignorant of scripture try to force meaning into pieces of scripture like this to gain support for their own opinions all the time. This is why we have so many different versions of Christianity and so many different Christian-based sects that are not actually Christian at all.

Do you see why it may take a very long time to figure out God's reasoning? In Genesis 30, Jacob (Israel) has a son named Joseph. Joseph's brothers get jealous, want to kill him, and end up selling him into slavery. While enslaved in Egypt, he becomes second to the Pharaoh in power and authority because he could essentially predict the future, specifically about a famine. Years pass; famine arrives. Joseph's brothers come to ask for grain from the Pharaoh. They do not recognize Joseph, so Joseph messes with them quite a bit before revealing himself to his brothers. This is a very entertaining piece of scripture that I love—a little playful, mental revenge before a very heartwarming reunion with his family after years of separation. His brothers break down and cry, begging for his forgiveness. He forgives them and then says one of the most impactful and beautiful speeches in the Bible.

> Then Joseph said to his brothers, "Come close to me." When they had done so, he said, "I am your brother Joseph, the one you sold into Egypt! And now, do not be distressed and do not be angry with yourselves for selling me here, because it was to save lives that God sent me ahead of you. For two years now there has been famine in the land, and for the next five years there will be no plowing and reaping. But God sent me ahead of you to preserve for you a remnant on Earth and to save your lives by a great deliverance. "So then, it was not you who sent me here, but God. He made me father to Pharaoh, lord of his entire household and ruler of all Egypt." *(Genesis 45:4–8 NIV)*

Is this not beautiful? He is essentially telling his brothers that while what they did, they did for evil, God meant it for good (which is restated in Genesis 50:20). This is a very comforting verse that shows how sovereign and amazing God is. Through faith, we are saved, and through faith, we are comforted.

Find that which is bad in your life's past, find the source of the depression or at least the spike of your depression. Once you isolate this event, look for what's positive in that situation. Look for a positive outcome that is concealed by the negatives. Dig deep into the event until you see what you need to learn. For me, I needed to learn a few things.

The first thing I had to learn was that I can't trust people and can only trust God. The second thing I needed to learn was that I can't control everything. When I realized and accepted that I can't control everything, my night terrors subsided; I stopped having that recurring nightmare. This is what the dream was trying to tell me: I'm not in control. Do you know why I accepted this challenging truth? I did it because the one I do trust… He's in control of everything.

Again, don't focus on seeing God's reason; focus on forgiving those who hurt you (including yourself). Once you've forgiven, once you've released that blame, once your soul is free from the prison of holding a grudge, then and only then will you be able to move on and experience a chance at joy.

> Bear with each other and forgive one another
> if any of you has a grievance against someone.
> Forgive as the Lord forgave you. *(Colossians 3:13 NIV)*

# Read the Bible

You should have been able to see this coming; the second step is to read your Bible. Should you read it cover to cover? Should you bounce around from book to book? Should I start in the New Testament? Good questions; the answer is yes.

Have you ever read the Bible before? If not, I'd recommend you start in the book of Matthew, read the entire New Testament, then start over from Genesis, and then read it cover to cover. The reason I'd recommend it this way is so that you can be sure to clearly understand the biblical Gospel that is presented in the New Testament. Once you understand the Gospel as Jesus himself taught it, then you're ready to begin diving into the Old Testament. To make this very clear and straightforward right away, allow me, if you will, to share the biblical Gospel with you right now.

You've probably heard the story of Adam and Eve. God makes the world, he makes humans, humans get tempted by the devil to disobey God, humans sin by disobeying God, that sin separates us from our creator, and we become the enemies of God. Sucks, right? "But I thought we were all God's children?"

Simply put…no. Humans are all the creation of God, just like everything else, but not all humans are the children of God. The Bible explains that when we are saved, we are adopted as the children of God *(Galatians 4:5, Romans 9:8, Ephesians 1:5, Romans 8:14–17)*. So how do you get saved? That's also simple. The requirement for entering heaven is perfection. Are you perfect, or are you a guilty sinner just like me and every single person who has ever walked on the face of this earth (aside from Jesus)? You're a sinner; you're a terrible, blasphemous, lying, rebellious, murderous, coveting thief… just like me. The Bible says that if you fail in one area of the law, you are guilty of all of it. *But, like, I'm not as bad as some people*, you think using a very incorrect logic. You see, we aren't being graded on a curve; we aren't compared to other people—we are compared to God. So do you admit to yourself that you're a sinner? If yes, you're being honest with yourself. If not, you're lying to yourself, which is a sin. So now you can admit it, right? If ever you'd lied, if ever you'd stolen something even if it was as minor as downloading a song illegally, if ever you have said God's name in vain, if ever you have hated someone, if ever you have cheated, if ever you have desired to have something that belonged to someone else…if ever you have done any single one of those, you're a sinner and you have earned the death penalty, just like me.

The Bible says that the wages of sin is death *(Romans 6:23)*. What this means is that we earn death by doing things that God finds repulsive and evil. This is why we die…it's because we sin. We can't help but sin. We love sin because we are human. The Bible says that we love darkness (sin), and so we fear the light (God) because in the light, our evil deeds will be exposed *(John 3:19-20)*. Though we are the enemies of God, God loves us so much that He became a person, He lived a perfect, sinless life, and then He died a brutal death so that He could take our punishment for us. Jesus is the Son of God, God in the flesh, fully God and fully man. Jesus said that He is the way, the truth, and the life and that no one may come to the Father except through Him. Jesus said that all you have to do is believe in Him, and He will give you everlasting life as a free gift. It's not based on works, how good you can be, or anything else; it's God's loving grace and His underserved mercy *(John 3:16, Ephesians 2:8–9, 2 Corinthians 5:21, John 1:1–14, John 14:6)*.

By sinning, we broke God's law, but Jesus paid our fine so that we can spend eternity with Him. The only alternative to this is Hell. You've heard of Hell, the Lake of Fire, but what you might not know about Hell is that it is called the second death *(Revelation 20:14)*. This is where our souls go to die if we are not saved. That is why heaven is referred to as eternal life because though our bodies may die, our souls won't.

To reiterate, we sinned, God came to earth as Jesus to pay for our sins, all we have to do is put our trust, our faith in Him alone, and we are saved. How beautiful is that? Every religion that has ever existed has had what's called a works-based salvation where their religion teaches them that they have to do good enough to reach their version of heaven—that's how you can tell it's a false religion. Christianity is the only belief system that has ever existed that is *faith alone*. There are some religions like Mormonism, Catholicism, and the Jehovah's Witnesses (JWs) that call themselves Christian but have different gospels or even different gods altogether. For example, the Bible says that Jesus is God **(John 1:1)**; the JWs and Mormons say that God created Jesus. The Bible says it is by grace that we are saved through faith, not based on works, just the gift of God *(Ephesians 2:8-9)*; Catholics, Mormons, and JWs say that it's based on faith *plus works*. Why is this a big deal? Well, it's a big deal because the Bible says there is only one real Gospel, and it's salvation through faith alone in Christ alone. The Bible very specifically states that anything different than this Gospel cannot save you.

I am astonished that you are so quickly deserting the one who called you to live in the Grace of Christ and are turning to a different gospel—which is really no gospel at all. Evidently some people are throwing you into confusion and are trying to pervert the Gospel of Christ. But even if we or an angel from Heaven should preach a gospel other than the one we preached to you, let them be under God's curse! As we have already said, so now I say again: If anybody is preaching to you a gospel other than what you accepted, let them be under God's curse! *(Galatians 1:6–9 NIV)*

And if by grace, then it cannot be based on
works; if it were, grace would no longer be grace.
*(Romans 11:6 NIV)*

Okay, so now that we understand the Gospel, read it for yourself. The Bible isn't a book of fairy tales with rainbow butterflies and unicorns; everything in the Bible is real, and there is a lot of dark stuff in the Bible, so don't take it lightly. The Bible is history as well as prophecy as well as poetry and philosophy as well as war stories and horror stories as well as inspiration and the means of true salvation. It is the Word of God, His love letter to us so that we can know Him… so that we can have a relationship with him.

If, on the other hand, you have read the Bible before, or at least some of it, start over at the very beginning and read it from cover to cover. There is a lot in there that might be seemingly repetitive and take forever to get through, but it's all very important. Do you have poor vision? Do you get headaches when you read? Do you just not like reading? Then download a Bible app on your smartphone; make sure you get one that provides you with a "Bible Verse of the Day" as a way to remind you to invest time in God's Word. On these apps, there are audiobook versions of many of the translations of the Bible. So throw in some headphones and have the Bible read to you. We are so blessed to live in a time with such amazing technology that allows us to take any and every version of the Bible with us everywhere we go. Let's take advantage of that blessing!

The next part of this step is going to be consistency: read the Bible every day. That's right! Every single day! Does that seem like a lot? It doesn't have to be! When you're driving, cleaning, or doing any other task that doesn't require you to listen to something, have the Bible read to you on one of the apps. Read at least one or two chapters every morning before you start your day or every night before you go to sleep. At first, this is going to feel like a chore unless you're like me and you have an obsession with the Bible and history. Stay consistent with your daily reading until it becomes habitual. Once it becomes a habit, it's going to get a lot easier, and you'll start to love it.

Another way you can make it more fun is to get a friend or a spouse or a significant other to do it with you! Hold each other accountable for the reading and make sure each person reads the predetermined amount each day. Then you can discuss what you've been reading and even start to dig into the weirder stuff in the Bible, like Genesis 6 or Daniel 9. Another option is to race one another. See who can read the fastest while still talking to each other about what you've read. Doing this will ensure that you are retaining what you read. Don't worry about spoiling it for the other person; it's not that kind of book.

So the other question that you might have right now is going to be, "Why the Bible? Why not the Quran or the Book of Mormon or some other book?"

That's a good question, and it has a good answer as well. The Bible was written over the course of approximately 1,500 years by over forty different scribes from three different continents, in three different languages (Hebrew, Greek, and Aramaic). The vast majority of the writers never met one another, and yet when it all came together, it all said the same thing. It talked about the one true God (Yahweh), it talked about the coming Messiah, it talked about the future, the past, and it never contradicted itself. God is the author of the Bible and used many writers to create what we now have as the Bible. The Bible is inerrant, which means there are no flaws in it. There isn't a single part of the Bible that can be disproven, there isn't a single part of the Bible that contradicts itself (in its original language), and there isn't a single false prophecy. The Bible has a hundred-percent accuracy rate in predicting the future. That's amazing and impossible, all of that is. There isn't a single other book that has ever been constructed that can come close to the Bible.

People will be confused and think the Quran talks about the same god, and it doesn't. The God of the Bible gives us his name, which is Yahweh. The Bible says there is no God besides Yahweh *(Isaiah 43:10, 44:6)*. The Quran, however, says there is no god but Allah. Now some people think Allah means god. This isn't true. The Arabic word for god is *illah*. The passage that I'm referencing in the Quran states there is no illah (god) but Allah (name of a specific god). That, and it's full of false prophecies, and its history has been disproven. The Book of Mormon was written by a con artist who had an extensive criminal history for fraud and even witchcraft. Joseph Smith had well over seventy documented false prophecies and led people after a different god than the one in the Bible. The Bible says that if any "prophet" has a single false prophecy or leads you after a different god, you can know that they are a false prophet and that they are a tool of the devil *(Deuteronomy 18)*.

So that is an extremely brief explanation of why the Bible is the only real form of scripture. Though I could write entire books on that single subject, I will leave it there to make this simple. So how do you make reading the Bible a habit, as we mentioned before? Well, psychologically, a habit is formed after doing something for thirty days. Once you hit the thirty-day mark, it'll be a habit, and it won't feel like a chore anymore. So give yourself the challenge to read at least one to two chapters every day for thirty days. Halfway through these thirty days, you should be able to see some effects of this start to happen right away.

How is the Bible going to help you? Well, it'll help in a few ways. First of which is that the more you read the Bible, the more you will learn about the God that made everything. The more that you learn about our wonderful God and His creation, the more you're going to start seeing the beauty in His creation; your perspective will change drastically. I have a very scientific-based mind, with a lot of my studies being on human muscular anatomy. As I started reading the Bible more, seeing the work of God became unavoidable and unmistakable. The complexity of a single muscle fiber contracting, not to mention hundreds of them working in unison to create a single movement that we don't even have to think about, is outstanding.

To give a simplified example of this, I present to you: this *paragraph*. Your eyes are made up of millions of light-sensitive cells that submit the light frequencies to your brain that then emits electronic and chemical reactions to process the images you're taking in through those millions of light receptors. After those signals are sent to your brain, your brain has to understand the shapes of the things that you see and then run the image through every memory you have in order to make connections to what you're seeing so that you can consciously realize what you're looking at without having to see what your subconscious mind is filtering through. Your brain then moves all of this information to a separate part of your brain so that you can remember what you saw as well as tie the information with a previous memory to create a memory base where it can be reassessed or triggered based on a singular variable or multiple variables.

What you just read is 944 characters, 779 excluding the spaces; that's 165 words that your brain was able to process in under forty seconds if you are a slow reader. With every word you just read, your brain has to not only associate an image with each character but also recall a generalized or specific definition of every word that you read. All this being done while your brain is making every small muscle contract to move your eyes from word to word while making your heart beat while making you breathe while distributing water and oxygen to every single cell in your body while digesting food while holding yourself up while focusing on this book and subconsciously paying attention to everything around you, all at the same time. That was a very oversimplified way of explaining how the thing you're currently doing that seems effortless is in and of itself nothing short of miraculous.

Our brains are just gooey balls of fat rolls encased with millions of neuroreceptors that both make, receive, translate, and process electrical signals and chemical emissions. There is a reason why we still know very little about how our brains work; it is so complex and mind-numbingly complicated (pun intended). We understand a lot about our psychology as we study human behavior, but psychology will always have a closer relationship to sociology than biology. We know a bit about how our brains send signals, what signals it sends, what areas of our brains become most active when we remember, when we plan, when we feel emotions, but we still know almost nothing about it on the broad scale of things.

I went off on this slight tangent because as I studied the book written about and by our creator, I started to see how miraculous his creations are—how amazing humans are. From a single spec of dirt to the oceans to every creature on earth to every atom in every molecule, God placed every individual one for a specific reason. All of this to say, God made you very specifically, very carefully, and very purposefully. Ephesians 2:10 tells us that God created a plan for us and a set of good works that he wants to accomplish through us. Some people focus too much on this, where we start to worship the creation rather than the creator. This is obviously bad. Don't love the world, but instead love the one who created it simply by speaking it into existence.

Now this isn't saying not to love people; in fact, we are commanded to love each other *(Matthew 22:37-39)*. What I'm expressing is that we should love nothing more than how much we love God. Jesus said that we must hate the world and hate our families in comparison to how much we love Him *(Luke 14:26)*. So how can we love Jesus more than anything? Well, it all starts with reading His love letter to us—the Bible.

# Prayer

Now this step, I'm going to spend a bit of time on the specifics of how to pray according to the Bible. A lot of those who are reading this who are currently battling with depression maybe have never prayed, maybe don't know how or even understand what prayer is. Many religions have different versions of prayer, from thinking you have to pray in a specific language, in a nonexistent language, repeat a prewritten prayer multiple times, etc.

So how should you pray? Well, let's look at the Bible. Jesus gave us a template that has been since named the Our Father prayer. This prayer was never meant to be repeated, as it's done in some religions that are loosely based on Christianity. Roman Catholicism, for example, will demand that its subjects recite prewritten prayers like the Rosary, Our Father, or Hail Mary prayers after confession to regain forgiveness or obtain more grace for the sins of that past week, month, year, or even decade. If you recall, in the previous chapter, when we went over the Gospel, we saw that the Bible says it's salvation through faith alone in Christ alone. No works to regain forgiveness. The Bible says that Jesus made us holy through His single sacrifice *(Hebrews 10:10)* so that we are no longer slaves to the law (works).

The reason Jesus gave us this template was just as an example of how to pray. Matthew 6:9-13 (NIV) says,

> This, then, is how you should pray: "Our Father in heaven, hallowed be your name, your kingdom come, your will be done, on Earth as it is in heaven. Give us today our daily bread. And forgive us our debts, as we also have forgiven our debtors. And lead us not into temptation, but deliver us from the evil one."

Let's dissect these verses, shall we? Right off the bat, Jesus says, "This is how you should pray," setting it up to be an example. It is then followed by addressing God the Father specifically to be the one you pray to. Not to angels, not to dead people, not to Jesus, but to God the Father through Jesus. He follows the address to God the Father by saying, "Hallowed be your name." This is essentially praising God, saying that his name is holy and beautiful and blessed. After this, it's praying not for our wants but for God's wants. "Your will be done" is such an overlooked beautiful aspect of this that not many people pay enough attention to. This is reiterated in James 4, where James, the biological brother of Jesus (Son of Mary and Joseph), says, "You ought to say, 'If it is the Lord's will, we will live and do this or that.'"

This is also stated by Jesus when He is praying to the Father as the hour of his crucifixion approached.

> "Abba, Father," he said, "everything is possible for you. Take this cup from me. Yet not what I will, but what you will." (Mark 14:36 NIV)

> Father, if you are willing, take this cup from me; yet not my will, but yours be done. *(Luke 22:42 NIV)*

Jesus is the second person of the trinity of God: the Father, the Son, and the Holy Spirit. Jesus humbled Himself to such an extent that He submits Himself to the Father's will. That's amazing. He did that partially to show us that we must be humble and submit ourselves to God and do whatever accomplishes God's will.

"Give us today our daily bread," such a humble request, asking that God will provide us with what we need. If we don't eat, we die. So praying to win the lottery or something like that, it's not a necessity. Am I saying don't pray for that? Of course not! That would make me a hypocrite! I've prayed countless times to win the lottery, but every time that I prayed for it, I prayed, "If it's your will, God, then please let me win this."

We have to understand that praying to God isn't like summoning a genie. God doesn't grant wishes. He takes what we want into consideration, but ultimately we have to remember it's His will, not ours. So remember that when you pray, sometimes the answer is no. "Forgive us our debts, as we also have forgiven our debtors," what does this mean? Well, if you remember from step 1, the part about how if we forgive others, God will forgive us—this is what that is talking about. So what is our debt? Well, if "the wages of sin is death" *(Romans 6:23)*, then this would be the debts that were owed and forgiven of. God forgives us of our sins that we commit against Him *(Psalm 51)*, as we must forgive those who have sinned against us. Those who have lied to us, hurt us, neglected us, abused us, made us feel terrible in every sense of the word, we must forgive them as Jesus would. Remember, the goal of this is to become more like Jesus, so we need to imitate him on every possible level.

"Lead us not into temptation, but deliver us from the evil one," this is powerful. Now while we will be forgiven of all of our sins, the Bible makes it very clear that we must avoid it at all costs. Jesus said, "And if your right hand causes you to stumble (sin), cut it off and throw it away. It is better for you to lose one part of your body than for your whole body to go into Hell" *(Matthew 5:30 NIV)*. Another example can be found in the writings of Paul to the Corinthians, which would be, "Everything is permitted, but everything isn't beneficial. Everything is permitted, but everything doesn't build others up" *(1 Corinthians 10:23 CEB)*. So while we could do everything, we shouldn't because it just makes us a hypocrite, and it displeases

God. God is our Heavenly Father; we need to do everything we can to make him proud.

Now I understand that for a lot of you, you may have had a bad relationship with your biological father or maybe never even knew him. Maybe your dad was neglectful, abusive, violent; maybe he abandoned you. Due to situations like this, some people have a negative opinion of fathers. Let me assure you, God isn't your dad. God will never lie to us, God will not abandon us, God will not hurt us, and God will not forget us. God is the perfect Father. He's not sinful; He's loving and full of mercy and grace, compassion and truth, wisdom and knowledge.

God is great, and He loves you. Whether you are a Christian or not, He loves you. That's why He sent Jesus. He loves you and gave you a way to spend eternity with him. I can't possibly imagine something more beautiful than spending a second, let alone eternity, with our Creator. God wants everyone to be saved *(1 Timothy 2:4)*, but He is just, which is why not everyone will be saved. Only those who accept the one true biblical Gospel of "faith alone in Christ alone" will be saved.

Back to the Our Father prayer, the part about delivering us from the evil one is just as heavy as keeping us away from temptation. The evil one that is referenced is who you would know of as Satan. He is the evil one referred to often in the Bible. Satan is not the only evil spirit, but the Bible does seem to give him a lot more attention than any other fallen angel/demon. So it is good to pray that we stay away from him and will be delivered from him. Now some people think that we should fear the devil; I'd like to show you biblically why we shouldn't fear the devil and why, simply put, if you are a Christian, neither Satan nor any other demon can touch you, period. Jesus is our protection against evil. When we put our complete trust in Jesus, we put on the armor of Christ to protect us in this spiritual battle against any and all evil spirits (fallen angels/demons).

The seventy-two returned with joy and said,
"Lord, even the demons submit to us in your
name." He (Jesus) replied, "I saw Satan fall like

lightning from heaven. I have given you authority to trample on snakes and scorpions and to overcome all the power of the enemy; nothing will harm you. However, do not rejoice that the spirits submit to you, but rejoice that your names are written in heaven." *(Luke 10:17–20 NIV)*

This is so cool. I'm smiling while writing this just as I smile when I read that. Seriously, how cool is that? Jesus says that we shouldn't rejoice about having power over evil spirits but instead to rejoice because we are saved! That's just so beautiful and so powerful. So while we cannot be harmed by any evil spirit, Jesus says that's so minor compared to us being redeemed from this sinful world and being promised that we will live eternally with God! Ugh, I love this!

Finally, be strong in the Lord and in his mighty power. Put on the full armor of God, so that you can take your stand against the devil's schemes. For our struggle is not against flesh and blood, but against the rulers, against the authorities, against the powers of this dark world and against the spiritual forces of evil in the heavenly realms. Therefore put on the full armor of God, so that when the day of evil comes, you may be able to stand your ground, and after you have done everything, to stand. Stand firm then, with the belt of truth buckled around your waist, with the breastplate of righteousness in place, and with your feet fitted with the readiness that comes from the Gospel of peace. In addition to all this, take up the shield of Faith, with which you can extinguish all the flaming arrows of the evil one. Take the helmet of salvation and the sword of the Spirit, which is the word of God. And pray in the Spirit on all occasions with all kinds of prayers and requests. With this in mind,

> be alert and always keep on praying for all the
> Lord's people. *(Ephesians 6:10–18 NIV)*

If reading that didn't make you smile just a little bit, I'm not sure what will. Scripture is so poetic and beautiful sometimes. It's such a wonderful and fitting metaphor about preparing ourselves for this spiritual war that we find ourselves in. Depression is just like that. It's a war; it's a battle every single day to try to get out of bed, go to work, go on with our seemingly monotonous lives of repetition. So instead of just sitting back and dealing with it, let's put on the armor of Christ. Let's fight back against this evil and fight vigorously against the evil one. Let's present our request to God for him to take this pain away from us, for him to save us from this depressive state of mind. In other words, *let us pray.*

So I've shown you some biblical stuff on how to pray, but now I'd like to explain in more depth on things you should do when you pray as well as things you should never do. It's not me that's making this up, nor is it my opinion; it's what the Bible says, so if you hear something that goes against what you've been taught, are you going to trust the Bible or your tradition?

> In vain do they worship me, teaching as
> doctrines the commandments of men. You leave
> the commandment of God and hold to the tradi-
> tion of men. *(Mark 7:7–8 ESV)*

I am blessed to have developed a humility to the Bible. If ever I think something or have learned about something that was *in* the Bible and then later learn that it's not in the Bible, or worse yet, if the Bible specifically forbids it, I'll abandon that traditional belief immediately. If it contradicts the Bible, it's not from God, period.

> All Scripture is given by inspiration of God,
> and is profitable for doctrine, for reproof, for
> correction, for instruction in righteousness, that
> the man of God may be complete, thoroughly

equipped for every good work. *(2 Timothy 3:16 NKJV)*

So one very important part of praying is knowing whom to pray to and whom to pray through. Some traditional beliefs that stem from pagan religions will lead people to think they can pray to dead people or saints; this isn't true. Some people think you can pray to angels; this is also not true. In fact, both of those are forbidden. See, praying is at its core, a beautiful and personal form of worship. If you were to pray to Mary, for example, you're worshiping her. That's evil because it's worshiping something besides God, which would be idolatry. Add to that the fact that Mary is dead, and it also becomes necromancy. The forbiddance of idolatry is the second commandment of the Ten Commandments given to Moses by God in the book of Exodus *(Exodus 20:4-5)*. Idolatry is worshiping something or someone besides God or trying to make a god in your head that suits you better than the one true God of the Bible. If someone says, "To me, I think god is like…," stop them right there because no—God, through scripture, told us exactly who he is. If your image of God doesn't match with the way he revealed himself to us, then you have a false god, and that is idolatry. To make it worse, the Bible actually says that when you do worship an idol, you are actually worshiping something, but that something is a demon.

What am I saying then? That an idol is anything, or what is offered to idols is anything? Rather, that the things which the Gentiles sacrifice they sacrifice to demons and not to God, and I do not want you to have fellowship with demons. You cannot drink the cup of the Lord and the cup of demons; you cannot partake of the Lord's table and of the table of demons. *(1 Corinthians 10:19-21 NKJV)*

Now some people that pray to Mary will say, "Oh, we don't pray to Mary. We just ask her to intercede/mediate our prayers for us." The problem with this is that…no. Mary is dead; she cannot hear you. The Bible explains that when we die, we have no contact with the earth. On top of this, the Bible specifically says that the *only* mediator between God and us is Jesus.

> For there is one God and one Mediator between God and men, the Man Christ Jesus. *(1 Timothy 2:5 NKJV)*

This leads us into the most important part—the mediation. Jesus is our mediator, our only mediator, so it's through Jesus that we must pray. We pray to God the Father, through Jesus. Not *to* Jesus but *through* Jesus. You may have heard, when some people pray, they will say, "In Jesus's name I pray. Amen." This is the proper way to pray. We pray to our Heavenly Father in Jesus's name.

> Whatever you ask in My name, this I will do, that the Father may be glorified in the Son. *(John 14:13 ESV)*

Jesus's death gave us a beautiful open channel to communicate directly to God. In the Old Testament days, people would need to go talk to the Levitical priests in order to talk to God; the priests would have to pray on their behalf. That's the way it was until about two thousand years ago. When Jesus died, the moment he gave up his soul, a massive veil on the temple ripped from top to bottom as a brutal earthquake occurred *(Matthew 27:51)*. This veil or curtain would be in place to separate the priest, who was in the Most Holy Place *(Hebrews 9:3)*, from the person who was in need of communicating with God. The significance of the veil ripping was to symbolize that there was no longer a need for a priest to pray for us because Jesus became our High Priest. Jesus entered the actual Most Holy Place so that He may intercede our prayers to the Father on our behalf. This is why Jesus is called the High Priest *(Hebrews 4:15)*.

Does this make sense on why we must pray to God the Father only and only through Jesus? Praying to anything or anyone else is idolatry, and that is devil worship according to the Bible. Prayer is one of the most personal forms of worship that we are capable of doing. It's the most sincere way to praise God, which is another reason why we need to make sure we only pray to God. The Bible makes it extremely clear that we must only worship God.

> Again, the devil took Him up on an exceedingly high mountain, and showed Him all the kingdoms of the world and their glory. And he said to Him, "All these things I will give You if You will fall down and worship me." Then Jesus said to him, "Away with you, Satan! For it is written, 'You shall worship the Lord your God, and Him only you shall serve.'" *(Matthew 4:8–10 NKJV)*

> Then he (an angel) said to me (John), "Write: 'Blessed are those who are called to the marriage supper of the Lamb!'" And he said to me, "These are the true sayings of God." And I fell at his feet to worship him. But he said to me, "See that you do not do that! I am your fellow servant, and of your brethren who have the testimony of Jesus. Worship God! For the testimony of Jesus is the spirit of prophecy." *(Revelation 19:9–10 NKJV)*

> Now I, John, saw and heard these things. And when I heard and saw, I fell down to worship before the feet of the angel who showed me these things. Then he said to me, "See that you do not do that. For I am your fellow servant, and of your brethren the prophets, and of those who keep the words of this book. Worship God." *(Revelation 22:8–9 NKJV)*

Now that we have discussed whom to pray to, let's go over what Jesus taught about how to pray. Jesus was very specific on how and where He wants us to pray and also how we shouldn't pray.

> And when you pray, you shall not be like
> the hypocrites. For they love to pray standing in
> the synagogues and on the corners of the streets,
> that they may be seen by men. Assuredly, I say
> to you, they have their reward. But you, when
> you pray, go into your room, and when you have
> shut your door, pray to your Father who is in the
> secret place; and your Father who sees in secret
> will reward you openly. And when you pray, do
> not use vain repetitions as the heathens do. For
> they think that they will be heard for their many
> words. *(Matthew 6:5–7 NKJV)*

So we see here, Jesus is making a stand against praying in public and praying in repetition. Jesus wants our prayers to God to be personal, like we are literally having a conversation with God. So don't pray simply so others can see you pray like the hypocrites that Jesus was describing, don't pray like it's a performance. Pray like you're having a private conversation with God because that's exactly what you're doing. Jesus mentions using vain repetitions in prayer, can you think of any examples of praying in repetition? Perhaps a prewritten prayer that is constantly repeated, like the Hail Mary prayer or even the Our Father prayer that we discussed earlier in this step? Those would be perfect examples of praying in vain repetition, and the prior would also be an example of idolatry.

So why is praying in repetition bad? Well, it's simply not sincere. Think of a child who has done something bad. Say, it's a little boy who hit his brother. His mom will get mad and punish him. In the process of punishing him, she will demand that the little boy apologize. So he will roll his eyes and mumble, "I'm sorry," until his mom is satisfied. Was he sorry? Of course not. When we are given a script to memorize and recite, we will do it without understanding why. The little boy will eventually understand the reason for apologizing and will do it in the future without being commanded to. However, that's not the way most people will pray.

Most people who are taught to pray in repetitive ways never seem to stop praying that way. They will just keep repeating prayers over and over their entire lives without ever thinking about the actual words they are saying or why they say them. Prayer must be sincere and from the heart. If every conversation you had with your spouse was scripted, how empty and bleak would that failing marriage be? Without honesty and sincerity in our communications, why would God even listen to us? We must worship God and God alone with complete sincerity and earnestness always.

Next, we must pray not only to ask but to thank. Make it a habit to thank God every time you pray. This will do two things. First, this will get you to humble yourself and tell God that you appreciate what He has given you—from the blessings as simple as having clean water to drink all the way up to thanking God for your friends and family. Second, this is going to make you start to actually appreciate the beauty in the world that God created. So no matter how small, thank God for at least one specific thing every time you pray. Try not to repeat the same thing. You could thank God for something as basic as waking you up, giving you air to breathe, eyes to see, a bed to sleep on, a roof to shield you, or even being able to read his Word.

So we want to ensure that we are praying to God and only God through Jesus and only through Jesus, privately and intimately and, above all else, humbly and honestly. God knows your heart, He knows your thoughts, and lying to God is not only a horrible sin but also foolish. You can't lie to the God who knows everything.

An honest example of the structure of how to pray would look something like this:

> Heavenly Father, I thank you that someone
> is reading these words right now. I thank you
> that you can use someone as little as me to spread
> your glory. God, I pray that you will bless and
> be with the one reading this prayer. I pray that

you will guide them through this book as well as Your Word so that they may find a new spark in life, a new hope for the future, and a new sense of joy and purpose as they give their lives to you the way I have. God, I pray that you will heal the one who is reading this from the sorrows that afflict them, from the pain that ails them, and from the crippling depression and anxiety that follow them daily. All of this I pray in Jesus's name. Amen.

# STEP 4

# Love Thy Neighbor

When asked about which commandment of the ten was the greatest, "Jesus replied: 'Love the Lord your God with all your heart and with all your soul and with all your mind.' This is the first and greatest commandment. And the second is like it: 'Love your neighbor as yourself.' All the Law and the Prophets hang on these two commandments" (*Matthew 22:37–40 NIV*).

What does it mean to love your neighbor as yourself? How do these two commandments summarize the rest of the ten? Well, if we take a look at the Ten Commandments, we can see what it means.

> Commandment 1: You shall have no other gods before me.
> Commandment 2: You shall not worship any graven image.
> Commandment 3: You shall not take God's name in vain.
> Commandment 4: Remember the Sabbath and keep it holy.
> Commandment 5: Honor your father and your mother.
> Commandment 6: You shall not murder.
> Commandment 7: You shall not commit adultery.
> Commandment 8: You shall not steal.

Commandment 9: You shall not lie.
Commandment 10: You shall not covet. *(Exodus 20)*

So how do those two summarize the ten? Well, if you love God with all your heart, mind, and soul, you're not going to worship anything or anyone besides God, you're not going to blaspheme His name by using it in a way that doesn't bring Him glory and honor, and you're going to remember what God has done for us. If you love your neighbor (everyone else), you're not going to dishonor your parents, you're not going to murder someone, you're not going to cheat, you're not going to steal, you're not going to lie, and you're not going to desire to have something that belongs to someone else.

Okay, that's all well and good, but how is it going to help with depression? Well, actually, a lot. When I first read this passage, I started to wonder what it really means to love your neighbor. It was a good thing I kept reading because Jesus explains it!

He asked Jesus, "And who is my neighbor?"

In reply Jesus said: "A man was going down from Jerusalem to Jericho, when he was attacked by robbers. They stripped him of his clothes, beat him and went away, leaving him half dead. A priest happened to be going down the same road, and when he saw the man, he passed by on the other side. So too, a Levite, when he came to the place and saw him, passed by on the other side. But a Samaritan, as he traveled, came where the man was; and when he saw him, he took pity on him. He went to him and bandaged his wounds, pouring on oil and wine. Then he put the man on his own donkey, brought him to an inn and took care of him. The next day he took out two denarii and gave them to the innkeeper. 'Look after him,' he said, 'and when I return, I will reimburse you for any extra expense you may have.'

"Which of these three do you think was a neighbor to the man who fell into the hands of robbers?"

The expert in the law replied, "The one who had mercy on him."

Jesus told him, "Go and do likewise." *(Luke 10:29-37)*

So what does it mean to love your neighbor? It means to take care of each other, help each other, be kind to everyone you meet; Jesus wants us to love other people the way that He loves us. This could be as simple as holding a door open for someone, helping an old lady across a busy street, or even just asking someone how they are doing in an honest and sincere way to see if there is anything you can do for them. This could also be as extreme as risking your life for them. Now I'm not telling you to run into a burning building to pull someone out, but if you are there and you're able to help, you need to love your neighbor as yourself. If you're willing to pull yourself out of that building, you need to be willing to pull someone else out.

Greater love has no one than this: to lay down one's life for one's friends. *(John 15:13 NIV)*

The point I'm getting at is this—help everyone you can as often as you can. Years ago, I was talking to this woman that I met out and about. We struck up a conversation, and she explained that she had just finished writing a paper for college on the idea that there is no such thing as a selfless act. She said that people only do good things for two reasons: they will get something out of it or make them feel better. At the time, I argued with her. I said, "There is a third option."

She said, "Oh yeah? What is that?"

"If you truly hate your life, if you are miserable and wish for an end to it, you might help people simply because you don't want them to feel as awful as you do," I suggested. She was stunned. She hadn't thought of that possibility. This is why the vast majority of comedians do the job that they do. They are depressed, so they try to make others feel happy so that random strangers don't feel as bad as the comedian. They tell jokes all the time to make other people feel better and forget their issues, even if for just a moment, so that the person doesn't have to be as sad as the one telling the joke.

She accepted that she was wrong and that this was a possibility. Now I see that she was also kind of right. After years of helping people with literally anything I could, telling stupid jokes and making terrible puns, I realized that I had started feeling better. Seeing them smile, seeing them happy became infectious, and I was surprisingly able to start feeling a little happier myself. So while my goal going into it was completely selfless, it evolved into something that became mutually beneficial.

When I'd help people, I never did it to make me feel good about myself. I never did it to try to feel like I was better or charitable in any way. I did it simply because I was miserable, and I didn't want them to be. Me starting to feel better was a side effect of helping, not the reason that I was helping. This was very noticeable for someone who was as obsessed with psychology as me, so I immediately started looking into it to find out why. Was it because I was obeying God? Was loving my neighbor really having that much of a benefit on me? Yes, yes, it was, but not for the reason that I initially thought.

Share each other's burdens, and in this way
obey the law of Christ. *(Galatians 6:2 NLT)*

What I eventually figured out was, I found purpose. I found the reason I was put on earth. I found that God put me here to serve Him by helping people. As I started helping people more and more, progressing further and further through my study of the Bible, I started sharing the Gospel with these people that I was helping. Many of the people that I've talked to about the Bible, many whom I've shared the Gospel with, have rejected it entirely. They've gotten mad about it. The flip side is that many people that I've been lucky enough to help have now heard the biblical Gospel. Whether they accept the Gospel or reject it isn't up to me. All I or anyone can do is plant the seed and pray that God makes it grow.

Are you starting to see why I'm specifying the Gospel so much in this? It's because though I have probably never met you, I love you. Love isn't some mushy emotion; it's a verb. Loving someone is an action. I love you, the reader, so much that not only do I want to help you break free of your depression so that you can enjoy life and feel better, but I also help you to establish a relationship with God through trust in Christ. If I am to truly love my neighbor and help them in their life but don't do anything to try to show them the truth about God and don't do everything I can to share the Gospel with them, then I'm not loving them. I not only care about your life, but I also care about your eternity.

The way that you can love your neighbor doesn't have to be the same way that I do it. Every person is unique and is blessed in specific ways. You might be exceptionally blessed financially and could monetarily help others. You could be like me, where you have spent your entire life learning as much as you possibly can so that you can be somewhat of a Jack of all trades. This has come in handy in so many ways. For example, I've spent a lot of time learning how to pick locks, which I know sounds nefarious, but trust me, it helped others.

One day, I was sitting at home after a long day of work when I got a call from a friend who had locked their keys in their car. So I went and *legally* broke into his car to retrieve his keys for him. Luckily it was in his driveway, so it wasn't much of an issue. Less than a week went by, and I got a call from the same friend. I held the phone to my ear, and before I could say hello, he said, "You're going to hate me."

I laughed and asked where he was. This time, it was in a parking lot, which made things more exciting. Now everyone who looks at you will guess about your intentions. It always helps to smile at everyone who looks at you while you are doing something that resembles a felony. My point is not that you should learn how to pick locks. My point is that we all have unique ways that we can help others.

Being physically able and in shape has helped in this regard as well, especially when someone's needs can be physically demanding.

There was a day when I was walking into the office building that my business is based out of that I looked at the main road to see a man's car break down. The only other person in the car was a child who was about four or five years old. The dad got out to push the car and had the little boy try to steer. So I thought for just a moment about the situation.

I had severely injured my hip the day prior and was walking with a pretty awkward-looking limp. So within a second that seemed to last a minute, I weighed out the options of causing further injury to my leg or walking into my office. Needless to say, my leg hurt a lot later that night. I ran in the most awkward way possible, almost skipping, to his car and started pushing while he went and got into the car to steer. Then I slowly limped back into the building for work.

A few months ago, I was hitting golf balls (badly) with a few friends of mine. I only had about three balls left to hit when a storm came out of nowhere. Rain and hail began murderously pouring down, almost as if to punish the ground we stood on. We packed up, got in our cars, and headed home. As I pulled into my neighborhood, I saw a man and his young daughter hiding under a tree. It was a brutal storm. As I pulled up to my house, only a block from where I saw them, I tried to figure out a way to help. *If only I had an umbrella*, I thought to myself before looking in my back seat and verbally announcing, "I *do* have an umbrella!"

I pulled my hood over my head and sprinted to them with the umbrella. "Hi! Here you go!" I shouted, hoping my voice would carry over the tyrannical hailstorm. The man said, "Thank you, but we are fine." I pointed to the street that looked like it was being filled with white marbles and then pointed to his daughter. "This isn't going anywhere, get her home," I said. He still wouldn't accept the umbrella, so then I handed it to his ten-year-old daughter and ran to my house to get cover. From my home, I looked out a window to see if they had left yet, and to my surprise, they were nowhere in sight.

A few hours passed, the storm faded, the sun broke through the clouds, and the doorbell rang. I slowly approached the door to find that man with my umbrella. I wasn't expecting it to be returned, but it was nice of him to do so. It turned out he lived pretty close by, so

I was literally helping my neighbor. I'm telling you these stories so that you understand it doesn't have to be some huge gesture; rather, it could be something as minor as giving someone an umbrella. Loving your neighbor is just that—you show them that you care through your actions.

Only a few weeks ago, I was doing some organizing around my house. Through the open window, what sounded like a gunshot rang out. I looked out the window to see a man standing over his bicycle with a newly flat tire. I stopped what I was doing and went out to my car, trying to mentally figure out how I'd be able to fit his bike in the back seat of my vehicle and give him a ride home wherever he lived. I pulled my car up to him and hollered out the passenger side window of my car, "Do you need a ride?"

He smiled and said, "No, I have a spare tube to fix the tire. My wife is going to bring a tool to get the wheel off." I looked up at him and said, "I've got tools!" He held his phone to his ear and told his wife, "Never mind." I popped my trunk open, grabbed my tools, and began removing his tire. As I was doing this, he stopped and said, "I recognize you." I looked at him, confused; I had no idea who he was. "You're the guy that brought me and my daughter an umbrella." I laughed, introduced myself, and went back to work on the tire. It was two small and separate events that significantly struck a chord in this man's memory.

One day, I was driving to get lunch when I saw this lady who was sitting on the sidewalk in a parking lot, holding a sign that said, "Homeless & Hungry." So as I went into the sandwich shop that I was going to get lunch from, I decided to buy an extra sandwich. I always keep a large package of water bottles in the trunk of my car, as well as multiple copies of the four Gospels of the Bible in my glove box. I pulled my car closer to her, collecting the sandwich, Bible, and water. I got out of my car and made my way across the street to the sidewalk she was sitting on.

As I approached her, a smile came over her face. She said, "Delivery? I love that!" I smiled as I knelt down next to her. Upon handing her the sandwich, she looked up in the air and said, "Thank You so much, God." She then looked at me and said, "I go to work at two thirty and I'm so happy I don't have to go hungry." I smiled as I continued to set the water next to her and proceeded to hand her the Bible. I said, "This is the Bible's four gospels." Before I could say anything else, she reached out to hug me and said, "Oh, thank you so much for the Bible and the food!" Then she made a comment apologizing for her smell. "Oh, I don't care about that," I said, laughing. Then I wished her a good day as I made my way back to my car.

Now here's one last story that I do not recommend anyone should ever duplicate. It was February second of 2016, and one of the worst blizzards I'd ever seen came on while I was on a date with a girl who was at the time my girlfriend. We had just finished seeing a movie and ran out into the already heaping piles of snow to clean off our cars. Now we drove separately. Had she been in my car that night, I would not have done what I'm about to tell you purely for the sake of her safety.

This night is still extremely vivid in my mind because it was in that snowy parking lot that I first told her that I loved her. I didn't even start sweeping off my car, just focusing on hers to get her out of there so she could get home safe before the storm got worse. I looked over at her, thinking of all we had in common, and the words just started battling my tongue. She looked up at me from her car, confused by the look on my face. "What?" she asked, smiling. I just shrugged. "You look like there is something you want to say," she said, walking toward me. I looked away and kept sweeping snow off her car. She continued her interrogation until finally I just said the words, "I love you,"

She froze in place (pun intended) while she thought about what I had just said. Eventually, she began moving again with tears in her eyes. So after a few moments of snowy kisses, she left, and I began sweeping off the snow covering my 1996 Honda Accord (which was a horrible car for the winter). After my car was sufficiently warmed up and swept off, I began driving home. I made it about a mile away from the theater before coming in contact with this hill…this steep and icy hill. *My car can make that*, I stupidly encouraged myself. I got halfway up the hill before my forward momentum was no longer with me.

I tried rotating my tires into different directions to gain traction but ended up being completely and utterly stuck in the road. Luckily there were no other cars around besides a snowplow that watched me suffer and then drove past me up the hill with the plow up. The driver didn't scrape any snow off that road, but his vehicle was heavy enough to make it up the hill. With no other cars on the road, I began reversing back down the hill until I started sliding and spinning down the hill. A smile creased on my face as I tried to figure out how I was getting home.

There was another road near the bottom of that hill that I had never traveled down before. Needless to say, it was more promising than my current option. I was driving down this road, covered in snow, and I was actually doing fine. I was making slow but steady progress until I ran into my archnemesis—another hill. I got stuck halfway up and couldn't even reverse now. I was on pure ice and could not move. I sat back for a moment and laughed, looking up as if to God, and said, "God, please help me get home. In Jesus's name, I pray. Amen."

Only another minute passed before I saw one of the most beautiful sights that I had ever seen in my life—a redneck in a large pickup truck with a deer guard. "You stuck?" he yelled from out the passenger window of his truck. "Oh yeah," I said, laughing. "You care about your rear bumper?" he asked. I thought for a moment about my already damaged bumper that got crushed from getting rear-ended a few months prior. "Nope," I announced with hope in my voice. He laughed and said, "All right, I'mma push you up that hill! You start gassing and don't let that car stop 'til you hit that light," he told me, indicating to the traffic light at the top of the hill.

I did what he told me, made it to the top of the hill, and had two choices: I could turn right or I could turn left to get home. I tried to think about which way should be scraped better, and then I turned left. As I started driving, I thanked God for that man and was just so happy that someone was there to help me. As my drive was progressing, I saw something awful—another hill. This one was steeper than the first two. I thought hard about what to do as I was getting closer and closer to the hill.

Out of nowhere, my eyes picked up on a man wearing a yellow winter jacket with his arm outstretched and his thumb pointing straight up. This man was hitchhiking at a bus stop. I paused for a moment to think about my choices. I could pick up this potentially dangerous man and risk dying, or I could try to make it up this hill in a car that didn't have enough weight. So thinking about the night's proceedings, completely content with how things were left off between myself and the girl I was currently dating, I had no regrets if I were to die. However, God gave us a will to live and gave me a brain that knew how to survive.

As I pulled over to pick up this random guy, I removed a knife from my back pocket, unfolded the blade, and placed it under my right thigh, just in case I needed to quickly take a stab at survival (yes, that was a stupid pun, but I'm not even sorry). He ran up, got into my car, and turned out to be such a nice guy. We successfully made it up the hill, thanks to his added weight in my car. As we drove, we came across a police officer that was out in the cold, helping a teenage girl with a flat tire in the storm.

"This is the kind of thing you don't see on the news," he began. "All you ever see are stories about cops on the news that try to make them seem like terrible people. That guy doesn't even have gloves on, and he is out there changing a tire for that girl!" I looked at the guy with an approving glare. We started talking; I asked him if he went to church and eased my way into giving him the Gospel. I got him home and eventually got myself home.

I do not recommend under any circumstances that you pick up a hitchhiker; however, I'm very glad I did and knew that was all God's plan. God wanted me to get stuck on that first hill so I'd take a different route. Had I made it up that first hill, the left or right would have definitely been a right turn. God sent a wonderful redneck to help me so that I could go on to helping another man out and sharing God's Word with him.

As you start to grow in your relationship with God, you start to help your neighbor and you start to share the Gospel as well; that's how you truly love God and love your neighbor.

> In the presence of God and of Christ Jesus, who will judge the living and the dead, and in view of his appearing and his kingdom, I give you this charge: Preach the word; be prepared in season and out of season; correct, rebuke and encourage—with great patience and careful instruction. *(2 Timothy 4:1–2 NIV)*

# STEP 5

# Set Goals

The next big step in beating depression is going to be the creation and pursuit of goals. These goals don't have to be something significant; in fact, I'd prefer that you set multiple little goals that can be easily achieved. Over time, these goals will grow to be much bigger objectives, and they'll develop into even more success. This is going to sound contradictory to what I just said, but make your first goal something that you will fail.

Did you assume the goal of this is to have little successes to boost dopamine levels in your brain by achieving minor victories? Not yet, it's not, but it will be. The first goal you set, I want it to be a biblical goal of biblical proportions. Make your primary goal to read the entire Bible, front to back, in two months. I don't know if you know this, but the Bible is very long. It's possible to read the Bible in two months, but it's a goal that you will most likely fail. Here's the thing—failure is okay!

Somehow down the line, we as humans have lost the gift of failure. When asked about his failures in attempting to create the light bulb, Thomas Edison said, "I haven't failed. I've just found ten-thousand ways that won't work."

This is the kind of mindset that we need to force ourselves to have. We need to view the positive side of every lousy occurrence, find the silver lining on every cloud. So say, you try to read the entire Bible in two months, two months will pass, and you might almost be

41

in the New Testament. I want you to count how many books of the Bible that you have read so far. Quiz yourself on what you've read to prove to yourself that you have accomplished something by retaining that information even if you haven't reached your goal quite yet.

The Bible contains sixty-six books. The Old Testament (OT) contains thirty-nine books, that's nine hundred and twenty-seven chapters. The New Testament (NT) has twenty-seven books, which are two hundred and sixty chapters. That combined with the OT containing the entirety of Jewish law, it takes a lot of time and patience to be able to read it and retain what it's teaching. Some books are very fun and interesting to read, like Genesis, the first half of Exodus, both 1 and 2 Samuel (which we will get into in Step 8), and Job. Some books like Leviticus are not as fun to read. Some of these books feel like they repeat the same things over and over. If it feels that way, that's probably something you should try to remember.

As the Bible explains lineage, it can also be pretty daunting. Listing names and relations that are extremely hard to follow can hurt your head a little bit. That being said, it's vital. So power through and pay close attention to every single line of the Bible.

While chasing this primary goal of reading the entire Bible in sixty-one days, set smaller goals to help you achieve this greater goal, as well as goals that have nothing to do with reading the Bible. Little, helpful goals could be reading one biblical book each day, reading at a specific time every day, drawing diagrams, or taking notes on what you read to help you remember critical figures and actions, etc.

Now for the unrelated goals, I want you to choose something that makes you better tomorrow than you are today. This could be working out, learning a new skill, finding a new recipe to learn how to cook, drinking a certain amount of water every day—something that will help with your physical health will always have a positive effect on your mental health (which we will get into during Step 9.) So think about what's important to you and go from there.

Are you overweight and want to get healthier? Awesome! Do that! It will help you in so many ways! Not only will you feel better physically, but your self-confidence will increase and, therefore, your love for yourself will increase.

Do you have a bad habit? Do you drink too much? Do you depend on nicotine? Is there another substance or activity that you find yourself addicted to? Maybe that smaller goal should be to reduce your consumption of those things. Do you have a few drinks every night? Cut it back to one per night. Smoke a pack a day? Cut back by one cigarette a day until you're down to only one a day and then quit. Are you addicted to porn? Keep yourself busy so you don't even think about it. Are you addicted to a harder substance? It's all the same. Reducing or quitting these bad habits/addictions will make you better tomorrow than you are today.

Don't have an issue like that? Good for you! Your goals can be different! Your goals can be literally anything! Are you bored? Is life just the same thing every day? Make yourself go out and do something fun. Go fishing or hiking, get a bike, learn to skateboard, rollerblade, or join a volleyball, tennis, racquetball, or basketball team at a local recreation center or gym.

It doesn't matter what you do; just do something that makes you better today than you were yesterday. Find something that you like, something that you find fun. Preferably do something active or thought-provoking. I add in the thought-provoking part because your brain is like the rest of your body—the more you work it out, the better it works. So if video games relax you, keep playing them. Some video games can be very good for cognitive development and critical thinking, as many studies have shown; the most nameable would be a study done by Oxford University.

The point of creating a goal is to get your brain and body working again in a way that is enjoyable and pleasurable to you that leads to a positive outcome. When you accomplish a task or achieve a goal, your mind will release a chemical called dopamine—this is the happy chemical. Upon smoking a cigarette, your dopamine levels increase, and that is why your brain associates it with feeling better or feeling happy (this is what causes the addictive tendencies). A study was done to show that a single cigarette increases your dopamine levels by 6 percent, while a line of cocaine increases your dopamine levels by 10,000 percent. This shows why some substances are much more addictive than others.

The overall purpose of creating these new goals and habits is to replace stagnation and bad habits. For example, if you're trying to quit nicotine, most people will end up gaining a significant amount of weight because they not only stopped taking an appetite suppressant (nicotine) but also began to crave sugary foods to help increase those dopamine levels. Sugar is horrible for you, far worse than nicotine by itself. This is an example of replacing a bad habit with another bad habit. We want to replace them with good habits despite how difficult it may be.

> I can do all things through Christ who strengthens me. *(Philippians 4:13 NKJV)*

Ending your chronic stagnation (not doing anything) is just as hard as quitting smoking. That's why we need little goals to help us boost the levels of naturally produced dopamine with healthy activities like exercise. Even with the exercise, set goals within it. Pick a long-term goal and then many short-term goals. Is there a specific weight that you'd like to be at? Do you want your arms to be a particular measurement? Make that the long-term goal and then make a ton of small goals to achieve it. If you can typically only do ten push-ups in a row, go for eleven. If you usually have dessert after dinner, skip it and eat fruit instead. Little goals that seem so minor will make the process feel a lot better because you will have these little victories throughout your day.

Remember throughout this that if you fail, that's okay! Look at and focus on what you didn't fail to do. You didn't hit your rep goal, but you went to the gym and tried; that's a success! You finished a book in the Bible: success! You helped someone today: success! You still smoked today but you smoked less than you did yesterday: success! These minor successes at positive goals will make your life pick up and help you start seeing the good, the positive, and the hope in life.

The goals I have had, to provide examples, are often ones that I have failed—not just failed but almost intentionally failed. Reading the entire Bible in a month, for example, was one that I failed. I got through it in the second month but couldn't make it in the first. I've set many goals in the gym that were both accomplished and failed. One goal was to do one hundred pull-ups and one hundred push-ups every day for a month, with the final goal being to be able to do fifty consecutive pull-ups. I partially failed yet partially succeeded. I achieved my goal of doing one hundred pull-ups and one hundred push-ups a day for three weeks until I injured myself in an unrelated event, which led me to fail the month and, therefore, fail to achieve fifty consecutive pull-ups.

So where did I succeed if I failed both goals? Well, not only did I lose weight and gain strength, but I also increased my average consecutive pull-ups from fifteen to twenty-five. In combination with that, half of the days, I was able to do all one hundred push-ups in a single set. I was okay with this failure because it still boosted my strength and endurance, and it made me better than I was before I started. Since then, I have lost a lot of that strength, so I will most likely reestablish these goals and try again.

A current goal that I have given myself is one that will take months or years to accomplish, which is increasing the circumference of my bicep/tricep from fourteen inches to twenty inches. This goal is one that I'm planning to fail. Twenty-inch arms on someone with my build will be extremely difficult to accomplish; however, failing to get twenty could result in me reaching eighteen instead. Even though the main goal can be failed, that doesn't mean the task was a waste of time.

I love projects and I love to stay productively busy. This doesn't mean busy work; everyone should hate that. I call it being productively busy because it isn't being busy for the sake of being busy. It is only for the sake of accomplishing a task that is ended by a goal. Projects are wonderful ways to achieve small or large goals. Be it in the act of fixing various items around the house or even doing artistic projects like painting or writing poetry.

It's on a nearly daily basis that I assign goals to myself despite how busy I already am. One goal I gave myself this morning was to read the book of Revelation again and write out a detailed summarization of each chapter to send to a friend who was asking me questions about it. Loving your neighbor can include accomplishing goals, and oftentimes it can be the source of a lot of these projects. I'm always willing to help people in my life and even get excited about doing it when it involves the completion of a project. Something as simple as replacing locks on a friend's house, swapping out a doorbell, mounting TVs, or even assembling workout equipment gives you small projects that are easy to accomplish.

The easier the goal, the faster you will feel both a sense of accomplishment as well as a want for more, a craving for another task. It's almost like an addiction but one that is very positive and beneficial to those around you as well as beneficial to your mental health. This will also increase your work ethic and kill that lethargic rodent that is constantly chewing at the back of your mind. However, these simple tasks will not be as rewarding as a tremendous goal. So set a larger goal with minuscule goals filling it.

This is why puzzle-like tasks can be wonderful. Even as simple as putting a shelf together. First, you must take inventory of the parts and tools. After that goal is accomplished, organize the parts based on the order in which they must be built. Following this will be the construction of the pieces until you arrive at the finality of having the shelf assembled and stable. Those who enjoy woodworking are prime examples of this, with so many minor tasks that must be done together and in the proper sequence to reach the desired result.

I strongly encourage you to try to make it through the whole Bible in two months. It is a wonderful goal that you might come close to accomplishing. Whether this is by reading or listening to an audiobook version of it, you're still spending time in God's Word, and that is going to be huge for you. The most important part of this is to pray for help with these goals. Ask God for strength and endurance to be able to achieve these goals, and you'll be amazed at what you can accomplish. Always plan out your goals to be aligned with God's will, and you will be overjoyed at the continued success that you will experience.

Commit to the Lord whatever you do, and
he will establish your plans. *(Proverbs 16:3 NIV)*

Now we are going to talk about something that might seem contradictory to my previous statements on setting goals for yourself to fail, which is in and of itself a contradiction. I want you to set a realistic goal that can be accomplished in a very long-term scenario. This goal should be one that you will refuse to fail in the task of accomplishment. It should be a goal that is nearly a passive goal, one that is to be set on the back burner and not be the primary focus, but rather it should be secondary at best. Something like this shouldn't be a goal for a career or a job. Something like this should be a very strong goal that is within your power to accomplish. A generic yet wonderful example could be blissful marriage.

A nonspecific goal to get (and stay) happily married is a wonderful one. Many people subconsciously put this as a secondary goal, living their life with hopes of marriage one day but inducing no real effort into the hunt for a spouse. The reason I'd say to set this as a long-term goal is so that you do not attempt to get a different time frame going. For example, if your goal is to get married fast, you will accomplish it. You could lower your standards and marry a desperate, dumpster fire of a person, but that will lead to unhappiness and divorce. We don't want that.

Marriage being the goal doesn't mean getting the wedding; it means keeping the relationship from the first date until the deathbed. This should be a secondary goal because the primary goals will be replaced by the secondary as time progresses. If you make this a primary goal, then you won't have the knowledge and skills needed to support and protect your family. So primary goals being the career and education would get you set up for success later.

Do not give yourself a time frame for this. Many people think they want to be married by a certain age. This mindset leads them into rushing into a relationship with someone who is truly wrong for them (most of the time) and resulting in a rapid divorce. Don't let time be the factor in your marriage; focus instead on the values of the person being the factor.

When you start dating someone, most people will start the first date off with very impersonal details such as pets, origin, family, hobbies, and work. These are fine subjects, but they should come second to religious views, morals, political views, and life goals. In many cases, most of these are very linked together. For example, if you are a Christian, you should never consider dating someone who isn't Christian. If you are a true, Bible-based Christian, you will uphold God's law as the standard for morality, while someone who is atheist will only be able to imitate morality.

True Christians that uphold this value for God's law will be indwelled with a value for human life, freedom, individuality, and putting God first. Therefore, Christians tend to be conservative. If for no other reason than the issue of abortion, Christians cannot be liberal and support the murder of unborn children. This subject is touchy and is a hugely important way to establish someone's morals.

For example, I'm American; on the first date I go on, I focus on determining the other person's morality based on religion and politics. Those two subjects that we are never supposed to talk about, those are the most important ones to discuss on a first date. If someone tells you that they are in the middle on a political scale, there are three questions that I will have someone answer to determine to which side they lean.

Are you progun or antigun? Are you pro-life or pro-choice? Are you for or against the death penalty? If the answer is progun, pro-life, and for…they're conservative. If they answer antigun, pro-choice, and against…they're liberal. If they answer this in a two-third fashion, the majority determines their political views and is a good indicator of their morality.

The reason for bringing this up is because values are the most important part of ensuring a relationship will last. I'm a Christian (duh) and a conservative, and I have dated my fair share of liberal women…never again. It's constant fighting and bickering and always leads to a relationship ending because your values aren't aligned. The Bible is the basis for a Christian's morality; without such, we can have no values that hold any value. Our values come from God and are therefore the objective reality of morality.

This is huge because if you are going to get married, Christ needs to be the center of that relationship from start to finish if you want it to succeed. With a unifying goal like sanctification in Christ and living for Him, you both will remain on the same page, the same trail, the same path in life and will be successful in making the journey together.

Living for Christ is going to be the ultimate goal. It will be the umbrella that covers all other goals. If you put Christ at the center of every goal and have Him be the purpose of the goal, you will find far greater success in achieving these goals. Let everything you do be done to praise God and watch His will engulf and captivate your life.

Jesus must be everything. He must be the epicenter of your goals, the engine that drives your motivation toward the completion of the goals, the fuel that strengthens your efforts, and He must be the reward that you find at the end of the goal. Let everything you do be done for God's glory and enjoy the side effects. As you do good, it results in good. There can be no better act of goodness than worshiping and glorifying the Creator, Designer, and Savior of everything and everyone. Guide every goal you have toward God and praise Him in every step you take, and there you will be able to find true success in life.

> For I know the plans I have for you,"
> declares the Lord, "plans to prosper you and not
> to harm you, plans to give you hope and a future.
> (Jeremiah 29:11 NIV)

Marriage, however, is just an example of a long-term goal. It could be something completely different for you. Just choose something significant that you would like to accomplish before you die. What's the point of a long-term goal? Simple, it adds purpose to life. The purpose of life for a Christian is to worship God and preach the Gospel. While this is primary for every single Christian, God made us unique with individual talents and abilities that contrast sharply with our neighbors.

Choose the goal that would be huge for you, something that will make you feel genuine joy and accomplishment. That way, you can be working on that in the background of serving God while giving you even more to live for. To add another very important reason for the long-term goal would be survival. For those who have dealt with depression in ways similar to my experience, suicide may be a constant thought that never wants to leave your mind. The tempting hope of relief from the struggling, stressful episodes of agony that we burden ourselves with through every waking moment of a seemingly monotonous existence can almost be the most pleasant thought possible. To escape from the mental prison that you have been living in. To turn off the lights so you no longer see the atrocity that lies before you.

How can we fight that seductive whisper of the noose, beckoning us to come hang out? How can we resist the soft and subtle comforting strokes of death's hand on our cheek? We must have something that is more enticing. That long-term goal needs to be something that you can truly look forward to because it will give you exactly that: something to look forward to, something to be happy about, a reason to keep going.

When your relationship with life is constantly getting interrupted with the temptations of death, the only way to keep that marriage strong is to love your life more. Death looks truly and unapologetically sexy in so many ways to someone who is deep in the darkest ruts of their personal pit of depression. As death lies before you in lingerie, holding a bottle of sleeping pills and a bottle of bourbon, it can be nearly irresistible to lean in and get a taste. But guess what? Death has herpes.

While death can seem so tempting at the moment, it's only going to lead to further problems. It's an all-or-nothing excursion into eternity that forbids us from ever returning to the life we married. Those who fall victim to this temptress are often those who don't know God. In such cases, their lives would be so much better, even if their life was pure agony and misery when compared to an eternity in Hell separated from God. While suicide is not a one-way ticket to Hell, as many false religions teach, most of those who take that path find that destination because they don't have their faith in Christ alone.

The question now isn't how can we make death seem worse... the question is, how can we make life seem better? Simply put: by making it more enjoyable and exciting. Go on trips, plan vacations, and reach out into the distant future and place the achievement of a goal that you are setting right now. A goal of mine is to have my tenth, twentieth, and all the way up to and past my fiftieth wedding anniversary. These are multiple long-term goals that stack on top of one another.

This goal works for me because it will give me a constant achievement to reach for. You aren't me, though. Make your goal something that you want. Something that will make you happy. Something so great that it will help you fight through the pains of life with enough ferocity to see that goal come to be reality.

Though death can look like a tempting, new, voluptuous lover, we must remember that being loyal to life is the better alternative. Life, while being familiar, can still excite us, can still surprise us, and can still please us. Every new journey in life can be one that is full of adventure if only you let your mind view life through that lens. Life is that stable lover that we have known since childhood. She's that girl that we saw ourselves growing old with. She's the one that is always waiting for you to come home, passionately enthusiastic to see you. As the saying goes, she can be a beach, but we love playing in her sand.

Life is a gift from God, just as Eve was for Adam and Adam was for Eve. God gives us such beautiful gifts in this world, none greater than His grace. We simply need to take the time and make an effort to alter our perspectives into letting us view everything as a gift from God. Looking back at the life I've lived thus far, I've been able to view everything as a gift, and I have thanked God for every single moment. The tragedies that I have lived through have actually been some of the greatest blessings I could have possibly asked for. Despite being disguised as a curse, life can be full of tremendous springs of joy that blend in with the hurricanes.

We all want our lives to be better, and keeping with the same metaphor, the best way to better a marriage is to spend more time together. Focus on life and make her feel special, and she will reciprocate the effort back to you. Life isn't the old ball and chain; she is the girl of our dreams that we must love vehemently. Love her with a passion and plan out the relationship with her so that the end looks even more beautiful than the beginning.

# Fake It 'Til You Make It

That's right! If you remember the prologue, I mentioned briefly this wonderful advice that I was given. I mentioned that I was about fourteen when I got this advice back before the primary issue that led to the most severe and damaging aspects of my depression. I mentioned that it helped but only a little bit. However, I did try again after I began this journey through the Bible, and it worked a lot better. Initially, when I got this advice, I was just a chronically unhappy kid who had yet to be damaged. Trying this advice out again after finding God increased its effectiveness.

So here is what you do: pretend to be happy. It's that simple. Smile, laugh, tell jokes, and act like you're happy. Not just around others, but even when you're completely alone and by yourself, act happy. This by itself will not work. This is something additional that, when combined with the previous steps, will help to start another positive habit in your life. This isn't me telling you to lie. I'm not telling you to lie to people and say you're happy and that your life is better. I'm telling you to act like you're happy and start to view things as if from the eyes of a happy person.

Does that make sense? I'm not telling you to trick people into thinking that you're happy; I'm telling you to trick yourself into thinking that you're happy. Again, this is only going to help you if you're already doing all the steps previous to this. If you came here expecting this to be a magical fix, that doesn't exist. There is no such thing as a magic pill that will cure you. This book is for those who truly want to get better, not for those who want the status of a victim.

Anxiety weighs down the heart, but a kind
word cheers it up. *(Proverbs 12:25 NIV)*

During the time that I was dealing with the metaphorical climax of my depression, at no point did I ever tell people about it or let anyone know I was struggling. There are two parts to this. The first part: maybe I should have told someone about it and sought out help. That could have been extremely beneficial for me in terms of my recovery. The other side is that I didn't want to claim that I was a victim. Everyone wants to claim they are a victim now so that they can uphold what they deem to be a higher social status because of a fictitious marginalization. This mentality is so stupid and dangerous.

Our society no longer values courage or honor; instead, we put the victims on a pedestal and emulate the moronic mentality of victimhood. This is partially why step 1 was to forgive whoever or whatever hurt you that led to a spike in your depression. If you accept that it's completely up to you now to fix you, then you can fix it. If you think that anyone else can play a part in where your life goes from here on a mental level, you will never get better. I don't want that for you. I want you to understand that regardless of what happened in your past, it's up to you and you alone to view the world in a more positive and beneficial light.

Do not be a victim of your own mind. Do not claim to be a victim of society or of a specific group. Instead, take responsibility for your own choices and your own situation and address it. Switch that mentality from "This happened to me" to "I let this happen to me."

This isn't easy in a lot of cases because if we put any blame on ourselves, then that means we are responsible for our own lives. If we have to take responsibility for our own decisions, that means people have to realize the decisions that they make are going to result in consequences, which is hard for us because we only ever want to blame other people for our lives' shortcomings. We rationalize tragedy to live in a bubbly, fictional world where we are always safe. People develop a mindset of, "This will never happen to me," "That kind of thing happens to other people but not to me," "That wouldn't happen in my neighborhood."

We get comfortable, and that leads to stupid decisions that have dire results. When the attack happened, what were you doing? Were you out late getting drunk? Were you walking through a dark alley alone? Were you in your house with the doors unlocked, upholding a false sense of security? Those are very small but real examples of how you can let yourself become a victim. The best way to avoid tragedy is to avoid the environments that tragedy loves to inhabit.

This is a sensitive subject, and I do not want my tone to be taken in an uncaring manner. My point with this is that people, all people, are evil and wicked at the core. If you think that most people are good people and there are just some bad ones, this is not only lying to yourself but also rejecting reality and scripture. People are mean, evil, selfish, and hateful by nature, period. Think about it, you who are reading this, you might view yourself as a good person compared to other people, but that is lying to yourself because the comparison isn't with other people. We are compared to God. God set the standard by which we must live. Compared to God, we are all awful and terrible people. You, me, our friends, the random people we see when we are out in public are all vicious, selfish sinners. If you still think most people are good, drop your wallet in a crowd and see if it ever finds its way back to you with everything still inside.

> What then? Are we better than they? Not at all. For we have previously charged both Jews and Greeks that they are all under sin. As it is written: "There is none righteous, no, not one; There is none who understands; There is none who seeks after God. They have all turned aside; They have together become unprofitable; There is none who does good, no, not one." *(Romans 3:9–12 NKJV)*

So where am I going with this? We can't trust or depend on anyone to keep us safe, to keep us happy, to keep us healthy; these are our own personal responsibilities. The choices we make intertwine with the choices of others, and that can lead to terrible outcomes. If you put yourself in bad situations, it increases your chances of getting attacked. This whole subject applies in both a literal/physical sense and in a metaphorical/emotional sense. You made a choice to be put into a position where someone can victimize you. Refuse to be a victim and take responsibility for your own actions, regardless of the actions of others.

Are you depressed because someone lied to you? No, you're depressed because you believed a liar. Are you depressed because someone hurt you? No, you're depressed because you let someone hurt you. Are you depressed because you were made a victim? No, you're depressed because you let yourself become a victim. So how do you prevent yourself from being a victim? Stop blaming other people and blame yourself.

Don't blame the other person; blame yourself. Is this saying to hate yourself for your decisions? No. This is telling you to take responsibility and change what you don't like. Do you feel like you're not pretty enough? Not tall enough? Not strong enough? Not skinny enough? Do those things make you sad? Do they contribute to your depression? Is that because of "societal constructs," or is it simply because you're letting evil people influence your opinion of yourself? Don't let that happen. Look at yourself through your eyes, not through the eyes of others.

Now, of course, there are specific scenarios that you may have lived through that were extremely damaging, so please do not think I'm reducing the impact of that tragedy; the previous aspects that I have mentioned are not for those extreme cases such as rape, abuse, molestation, and physical neglect (especially in juvenile cases). In these cases, you, of course, are not responsible for any aspect of the abuse or assault. That is true victimization. That being said, the past is the past, and we must move forward. This isn't to forget that it happened; this is going back to step 1, where you must forgive that it happened. From here, you can reestablish your goals, your wants in life and begin on down the road of recovery.

You are in charge of yourself, which means that you can change yourself. Your weight, your strength, your depression—you can fix what you don't like about yourself. You need to fix it based on what you like, not what others like. You are in charge of you. Do you want to fix your depression for someone else, or do you want to fix it for yourself? If it's not for you, you will fail. You must do things for your own sake.

If you quit smoking because your girlfriend/boyfriend wants you to, if you break up, guess who is going to go right back to the bad habit? Why does this happen so frequently? It's because you didn't quit for yourself; you quit for her/him. Which means it wasn't for your own good; it was just to try to please other people.

So back to the point of this step, fake it 'til you make it. Trick yourself into being happy by telling yourself that you're happy. Just like how thanking God for specific parts of life makes you slowly start to appreciate life more, I want you to look in the mirror every day, pick something that you like about yourself, and tell yourself out loud that you love it. "I love my eyes. I love my hair. I love my skin. I love my teeth. I love my arms. I love my legs. I love my laugh. I love my smile. I love my nose."

Saying these things will feel weird at first, but over time you're going to start believing the things that you're telling yourself because you know the things you say are true. How do you know they are true? You have a natural instinct to protect yourself because you love yourself. All you're doing is verbalizing it specifically.

Look in the mirror every morning when you wake up, smile at yourself, and compliment yourself. Over time, just this one thing is going to start making you feel happier. Act like this constantly throughout the day. Smile all the time, thank God for little things in your life like the weather, take note of the beauty in the world, tell yourself about what you see, and thank God for the food that you're eating, etc.

Constantly tell yourself that you're happy, and eventually, you'll believe it. This isn't to put on a show for those around you; this is to convince yourself that the change you desire to have in your heart is coming. Some people think that self-love is the most important part of life. This isn't true. Self-love leads to self-righteousness. I'm not telling you to love yourself for the sake of loving yourself; I'm telling you to love yourself simply because God made you. You are an image-bearer of your creator, designed to be a reflection of the glory of God, and therefore you should love yourself because God loves you. We must not worship the creation, but we must acknowledge that all of creation declares the glory of God *(Psalm 19)*.

This kind of thing has been the study of many psychological studies that I would highly recommend looking into. The psychology behind this is similar to positive reinforcement, but it will also help to build a positive habit. The amazing thing about our minds is that we will actually continue habits subconsciously without realizing we are doing them. This can be a beautiful gift but also a horrendous curse depending upon the habit. If you habitually think about the good things you see, that will be a wonderful blessing to continue to do so without having to think about making yourself view the world that way. On the contrary, if you only focus on the negative, you will continue to do so on a subconscious level. So it's vitally important to get these good habits going.

Again, however, we must be careful not to worship the creation, rather only the creator. We can be grateful to the creator for his creation but never think the creation gave us anything. God made you and everything in the world, and we must be grateful for everything created just because it shows proof of the amazing intellect of our creator. To clarify this further, be grateful for the creation, not to the creation.

You'll hear this kind of thing from naturalists, atheists, and New-Age spiritualists all the time. "Mother Nature gave us such a nice day today," or "The universe is on my side." No! That's worshiping the creation, that's idolatry. When I'd call someone out on this (in a loving way), the response given is usually along the lines of saying, "Oh, the universe is just what I call god." This kind of stuff deeply concerns me when I hear people who claim to be Christians say it. It usually leads to a conversation where they will essentially explain that they aren't really Christian. So it's a good time to share the biblical Gospel with them, since they may be confused about it or may never have heard it clearly. When I hear one of the New-Age spiritualists say it, I use it as an opportunity to talk to them about the real God. I'll usually start with a lighthearted jab along the lines of, "My God made your god," as a segue into explaining the difference between the creation and the creature and, from there, sharing the Gospel with them. So just be careful with this aspect of the step.

Fake it 'til you make it; trick yourself into thinking you're happy until you believe it. Don't let yourself be a victim. Thank and praise God every day for everything He has given you, and soon you will start to truly see the beauty in this world. That's step 6.

# Accept Jesus and Repent

Acts 17 in the Bible tells us that we must all repent. What is repentance? Repentance is when you truly forsake your sins and turn to God. This step is going to be very important in two ways. First, there is nothing more important than your eternal soul and what happens to you after you die. So repentance is obviously going to be huge! Repenting doesn't save you; in fact, it doesn't make a lick of difference for your salvation if done by itself. However, those who truly put their trust in Christ will repent as a byproduct. The Bible says that when we put our faith in Christ, we will be born again; we will be given a new heart, new desires. We will want to do what is right rather than what is wrong purely out of obedience to and love for God.

Before I was saved, my actions made no difference to me. I knew it was wrong to lie, cheat, blaspheme—I didn't care. Once I truly devoted my life, soul, and mind to God, I immediately wanted to be free of sin. Now the things I used to do repulse me. The thought of cheating or insulting God just makes me sick to my stomach because God changed my heart, and therefore, I repented. I begged God to forgive me, I told God that I'm putting my full trust in Christ for my salvation, I told God that I accept his free gift of Grace, and since then, I have been a child of God, and I know beyond a shadow of a doubt that when I die, I get to spend eternity with God.

The second benefit of repentance is that, once you turn from sin, you'll be surprised at how many bad habits are sinful. If you have an addiction, you are putting your addiction before God. I had a nicotine addiction for eight years before I realized that. I knew I hated being addicted to something, but I didn't know why. God changed my heart; he made me hate being addicted to this thing that made me feel calm and comfortable. I hated that I was addicted to it once I was saved, but I continued to be addicted to it for about six more years before I realized that I was putting nicotine before God. The first commandment tells us to have no god before God. Nicotine was my god.

When I realized that, I stopped almost immediately. The first few times that I attempted to quit, I failed. I failed because I was quitting for the sake of quitting. The final time that I attempted quitting, I was successful because I was doing it for God. I eased off it substantially for a few days to try to lighten the withdrawal symptoms that I knew all too well from previous quitting attempts. After a few days, I stopped completely. I went through just over a month of feeling physically sick, having migraines, being extremely short-tempered, and being very anxious. I remember praying to God multiple times a day, asking for him to give me the strength to resist the unquenchable urge to break someone's face on my knee. I was so mad at everything for no reason. I knew I shouldn't be.

Here's the callback to the previous chapter; I knew that it was all my fault. I put the full blame for the rage where it belonged—on myself. I made a choice to partake in a highly addictive activity. I made a choice to stick with it for years. I made a choice to quit and thereby give myself very bad withdrawal symptoms. It was my fault, so I knew I had to control myself. I didn't ask God to put a stop to the symptoms. I didn't ask God to stop the pain. I asked God for strength to deal with the consequences of my actions. I asked Him to help me control my anger so I wouldn't overreact when I dealt with frustrating people. I punched many random items during that month but never a person. God helped me through it, though it was all my fault.

Repenting of sin brings you closer to God because it's sin that separates us from God. Repentance, the turning from and forsaking of sin, does not mean you will never sin. It means you will have the motivation to avoid sin and a reason to do as good as you can. For those who think good deeds are required for salvation must consider this: the Bible says that our good deeds are filthy rags to God.

> We are all infected and impure with sin. When we display our righteous deeds, they are nothing but filthy rags. Like autumn leaves, we wither and fall, and our sins sweep us away like the wind. *(Isaiah 64:6 NLT)*

The terminology here for filthy rags by today's language would be the same as saying, our good deeds are like dirty tampons in the eyes of God. Graphic, right? As graphic as this is, it is so beautiful and poetic in the other aspects of it. This was from a prophet who was here approximately 750 years before Christ. He was explaining, even then, that we cannot be good enough to be saved by works. Even back then, it was salvation by faith, as exemplified by Job and Abraham.

> For the Scriptures tell us, "Abraham believed God, and God counted him as righteous because of his faith." *(Romans 4:3 NLT)*

We do not turn away from sin and do good things to be saved, so why do we do them? At multiple points in the Bible, it explains that the good works we do are not for salvation—they are for people. It is by our good deeds that we show the world that we are saved. We prove our faith to *humans* that we are true Christians. Some people would argue and say no, it's to prove our faith to God. Then you're not worshiping the right god. The God of the Bible knows our hearts, our thoughts, our intentions, and we don't need to prove anything to God. If I were to tell you not to do drugs while I leaned down to a coffee table to snort a line of cocaine, what would that make me? A hypocrite! The same goes for a Christian who says, "Don't sin," while stealing money out of an old lady's purse.

> In the same way, let your good deeds shine
> out for all to see, so that everyone will praise your
> heavenly Father. *(Matthew 5:16 NLT)*

I strive to practice what I preach. God commands that we be good examples for people specifically to reach them. If you see someone who seems to be full of life and has a palpable sense of joy about them who is doing nice things for other people, you would obviously be more inclined to listen to that man tell you about God rather than an angry man who is throwing rocks at little kids on bikes. It's the same concept. The unsaved person compares people to other people, which is why they all think they are good people. So when they see that a saved person is a shining light in a dark tunnel, it'll catch their attention.

> Prove by the way you live that you have
> repented of your sins and turned to God.
> *(Matthew 3:8 NLT)*

Those who don't know God live in sin constantly without a care for their actions even though their conscience tells them that they are doing something wrong. They just ignore the little nagging cricket. The little metaphorical angel and demon on their shoulders are always a tiny angel against a massive demon. Their moral compass always points south because they are still dead in their sins. They do not live a life dedicated to Christ.

> They claim to know God, but by their
> actions they deny him. They are detestable, dis-
> obedient and unfit for doing anything good.
> *(Titus 1:16 NIV)*

One of my favorite Bible verses states an explanation of why Christians are no longer dead in their sins, as well as gives more evidence that salvation is by grace alone through faith alone in Christ alone. The following verse is also very beautiful and gives a biblical backing for why we should continue to live.

> My old self has been crucified with Christ. It is no longer I who live, but Christ lives in me. So I live in this earthly body by trusting in the Son of God, who loved me and gave himself for me. I do not treat the Grace of God as meaningless. For if keeping the law could make us right with God, then there was no need for Christ to die. *(Galatians 2:20–21 NLT)*

Do you know what baptism is biblically? Being baptized is being born again. Spiritually we have died with Christ, we died to our sins. God raised us with Jesus. A water baptism is a symbolic practice that is a beautiful demonstration of our devotion to God. Jesus said to get baptized in water. He wanted us to have a public profession of our faith with that symbology. Why? For the same reason that we repent. So should we get water baptized even though it has nothing to do with salvation? Yeah! Absolutely! Why? For one reason, Jesus told us to. We repent because of our faith, just as we will be baptized in water to show to others that we have repented.

> This is the Good News about Jesus the Messiah, the Son of God. It began just as the prophet Isaiah had written: "Look, I am sending my messenger ahead of you, and he will prepare your way. He is a voice shouting in the wilderness, Prepare the way for the Lord's coming! Clear the road for him!" This messenger was John the Baptist. He was in the wilderness and preached that people should be baptized to show that they

had repented of their sins and turned to God to
be forgiven. *(Mark 1:1–4 NLT)*

Repentance is covered, so what do I mean by accepting Jesus? You may have heard the phrase "faith in Christ" without fully understanding what it actually means. I know it might seem self-explanatory, but I find that this is actually a huge issue of understanding among many people in religions that call themselves Christian. So let's first go over what a biblical Christian actually is to make this make more sense. As we covered in step 2, the biblical Gospel is that we are saved by grace alone through faith alone in Christ alone. So exactly what does this mean?

Grace is the free and unmerited, underserved gift of God to forgive us of our sins. We accept that gift by doing nothing more than putting our full faith in Christ. If you don't accept the gift, it's not given to you. If you try to earn the gift, it's no longer a gift and is therefore not given to you. This is why "faith plus works" religions have a false gospel and are therefore not Christian. So now that this has been covered, what is faith? Faith is trust.

When you're driving a car and there's a vehicle ahead of you that stops suddenly, what do you do? You stomp on your brakes to stop the car. You don't think about it, you don't try to figure out a different way, you don't worry about them failing, you simply trust fully that the brakes will work and they will cease the forward motion of your car. You don't realize that you're doing this because you're used to it. You put your faith/trust into your car's design. You trust that it will work. Do you know how it works? Some of you might, most of you won't, which means that most of you are putting blind faith in the people who made your car.

Putting your trust in Jesus isn't like driving a car and not knowing how its brakes work. God explained exactly how His grace works in His love letter to us. God has proven His existence time and time again. Just look around you, look at how beautifully designed His artwork is in every sunrise and sunset, every mountainous horizon, every snowflake that gently descends from the magnificent clouds in the sky. Now think about what you just did, your eyes, your brain, the thought process. The Bible says that the beauty of the world is a declaration of God's existence *(Psalm 19:1)*.

Trusting Christ means that you trust with full confidence, just like the brakes of your car, that your sins (all past, present, and future) have been paid for by Jesus and God no longer sees your sins. He now sees Christ in you. Trust the savior fully as confidently as you trust your brakes in your car or even as confidently as you trust a chair to support you when you sit down.

Okay, so you have put your faith in Christ and you trust that you're saved, what next? Now I want you to trust God with your life. Well, how do you do that? Same way. Stop worrying about the things you can't control and trust that God is taking care of it for you. Are you concerned about someone who is no longer in your life? Just present that request to God in Jesus's name to take care of that person and trust His will.

God's will is the most important thing to trust and depend on. Why? Because His will is the only thing that matters since it is the source of reality. If you think back to step 3, you may recall us talking about how we must pray according to God's will and even how the Our Father prayer states, "Thy will be done on earth as it is in heaven."

We pray that God accomplishes His will because what He wants is much more important than what we want. So what happens when our wants conflict with God's will? This is something that professing Christians will struggle with. You might pray for something and you might get a simple no as your answer. This might hurt your feelings, shake your faith, make you doubt God, and it would all happen because you are putting yourself in a position that says, "I know better than God."

Do you? You know more than the creator of wisdom? Hmm, all right then. Now for us honest people who humble ourselves in our ignorance compared to our glorious Father in heaven, we understand that God obviously knows better than we ever could even dream of. God is good and only good, which means His will is for the greater good and only for the greater good. When you were a child, you would get upset when your parents told you not to do something, even if it was for the best. You didn't understand and would blame your parents for your unhappiness. As an example, if you were trying to get a ball that rolled into the street as a car was coming but you were stopped by your parents grabbing you to prevent you from becoming part of the pavement, you would be upset that your ball got crushed and destroyed by the car without realizing that the car would have killed you. So you'll be mad at your parents until you grow and learn what actually happened.

It's the exact same way between God and us. If something doesn't work out in our favor, we will get mad, even at God, because of our own ignorance that prevents us from understanding the bigger picture. Think back again to step 1 when I told you about the old friend of mine who had gotten pregnant at the age of fourteen. Can you imagine the fear that she must've had? It must have been mortifying. I can't speak on her thoughts, on whether or not she was angry with God, or on how she viewed it. All I can speak on is the objective aftermath of the early pregnancy and how her life was saved by that beautiful blessing from God.

One thing I didn't mention in the previous recollection of this story was something that she did without realization of the impact. This girl gave her daughter the name Noah. She thought it was a pretty name, and it is. However, I'm not sure she understands how cool of a name that really is. Noah was a man chosen to be the continuance of life on earth when God saw that everyone else was evil and wicked. God commanded Noah to build an ark. Noah did as God commanded. Once he built the ark to the exact specs that God had given, two of every kind of animal came to the ark and got on board.

A flood came. The Bible says that the earth released the water that was in it, and the sky released the water that it held. People speculate on how that much water somehow came and went. Well, scientists have actually determined that there was an additional layer in our atmosphere compared to what we have now. This, as well as a surplus of water in the earth, would have been plenty of water to flood the whole earth. Then where did that water go afterward? Our best guess is that this is what made the ocean as we know it today.

After the flood stopped, the ark crashed on a mountain. The Bible's Noah saved life on earth, just as the Noah that I know saved her mother's life. God is so amazing, and His will is insurmountable. God's will was for her to live, and so she did by God blessing her life with a little lifesaver of her own. The feminine spelling of this name in English is Noa, which I think just drives the point home even harder that she spelled her daughter's name exactly as it is spelled in the Bible.

Trust that God is in control because God is in control. This isn't a self-defeating or circular argument; this is simply telling you to accept reality and trust the maker of reality, God. Do you put your plans as a priority over God's? I have another friend who was telling me about her disappointment and fear for her own plans. She is (at the time of writing this) twenty-four and has her mind set on the idea that she has to be married and have kids before she turns thirty (if you remember step 5, this is a horrible idea). This, in combination with having little success in the realm of dating, has left her feeling disappointed and worried. When trying to tell this girl the same thing I'm telling you about trusting God, she said, "It's hard for me to trust that God is good and wants what's best for me."

Immediately I replied with a question to confirm what she said: "You have a hard time trusting that the only being in existence that is good…is good?" I went on to explain that her premise is wrong to begin with. God wants what's best, not what's best for you. As an example of this, I brought up Paul in the Bible.

Paul was a Pharisee who hated Christians and persecuted them viciously until one day, Jesus made Himself known to Paul (who at the time was named Saul). Jesus blinded Paul and told him exactly what to do to regain his sight. Paul did this and immediately made a one-hundred-and-eighty-degree flip in his life and dedicated his life to preaching the Gospel. He spent his life being tortured, ridiculed, imprisoned, and ultimately killed for his faith.

God used Paul to reach billions of people. I say billions as literally as possible due to the fact that Paul's writings comprise most of the books in the New Testament. Paul lived a hard life for having faith in God. Paul is also the scribe of many of the books in the New

Testament. He was a mouth to preach God's word and a pen to write God's love letter. God's will wasn't Paul's will; however, due to his faith in Christ, Paul made his will line up with God's, being willing to be used to accomplish God's will. This is beautiful, and it is how we should all strive to live. If we align our will to match God's will, we will find that our plans work out much better because they are no longer our plans.

I want Paul's example to be lived out by all Christians. If you make God's will your will, you'll never be disappointed. Turn from your sinful habits and live your life for God according to His will rather than your own. That is step 7.

# STEP 8

# Write

Writing is going to be a solid next step in the process of beating depression. Why writing? Writing how? About what? These are the questions that we will answer in this step as well as how this step came from the Bible. To answer all of these, we need to start with a discussion about one of the most famous leaders who ever lived. More famous than any American president and more famous than any celebrity. We are going to talk about a young Jewish shepherd who became a king—his name was David.

In 1 Samuel 16, the prophet Samuel is told by God that he must go find a man named Jesse. One of Jesse's sons is to become the next king. Jesse shows up with all of his sons except for one. Samuel is confused that of the sons brought, he doesn't see the one God told him about. So he asks Jesse if he has any other sons. Jesse tells him that his youngest son is still out in a field, tending to sheep and goats. Samuel urges Jesse to send for him, and so he does. Once David arrives, he is described as a handsome man with dark skin and "beautiful eyes." Samuel anointed David as the next king, and the Spirit of the Lord came upon David.

The current King, Saul, needed David to come around, so look what God did.

Now the Spirit of the Lord had left Saul,
and the Lord sent a tormenting spirit that filled

him with depression and fear. Some of Saul's servants said to him, "A tormenting spirit from God is troubling you. Let us find a good musician to play the harp whenever the tormenting spirit troubles you. He will play soothing music, and you will soon be well again." "All right," Saul said. "Find me someone who plays well, and bring him here." One of the servants said to Saul, "One of Jesse's sons from Bethlehem is a talented harp player. Not only that—he is a brave warrior, a man of war, and has good judgment. He is also a fine-looking young man, and the Lord is with him." *(1 Samuel 16:14–18 NLT)*

Here we see God causing Saul to be depressed and giving him a solution for his depression, which was David. Saul loved David and sent word to Jesse that he wished for David to stay with him as his servant. Whenever the spirit would make Saul depressed, David would play his harp, and the spirit would leave Saul. David, however, traveled back and forth constantly between helping his father and serving the king.

Now a very important question that I feel obligated to address after that last verse would be: does God cause depression? This is not an easy answer to present, so bear with me as I do my best to clarify this. In short, yes and no. We see here that God sends an angel to Saul for the sole purpose of making him depressed and troubled. Yet we see immediately why God did that to Saul. We see that Saul calls upon David for this reason. Would Saul have called upon David to the extent that he did if not for his depression? Probably not. God doesn't do things without a purpose; He always has a reason. So we see some of the reasons for Saul's depression (we will see more as we progress through David's life), but does this mean that God causes all cases of depression?

In my specific case, as I mentioned in the epilogue, I was depressed and miserable as a kid before the crux of my depression came to be. Yet due to my decisions and choices, my depression was amplified. So in my specific case, I would say that God did in fact cause my depression. However, this isn't a negative. If it weren't for my depression, for my years of contemplating suicide, I don't think I ever would have become a Christian. I'll go in depth about my story in the prologue of this book.

The reason that I can confidently say that God blessed me with depression is because the outcome of my depression was God saving my soul. Maybe following the steps of this book can have a similar effect in your lives and get you to become a Christian. If I never went through extreme depression in my life, to a debilitating level, I would not have been able to write this book, which has the potential to help out a multiplicity of other people. I would happily go through everything that I've been through a second time if it meant being able to help others with the lessons that I have learned through my pain. If your depression led you to read this book, if this book got you to read the Bible, and if the Bible speaks to you and you become a Christian, then it's definitely possible that God caused your depression to bring you to Him.

That being said, humans are fallen creatures who are responsible for every negative affliction that we face. Our choices and our sins lead us into the illnesses and diseases that we experience, the bad habits and addictions that we fall prey to, and even the dark thoughts that haunt our dreams. We are to blame for basically every bad occurrence in human history, including most cases of depression. I'd say that if your depression leads to something wonderful for you, for someone else, or for the world, God caused it. If your depression leads to nothing positive in any capacity, then you can be certain that your depression is simply because we are fallen creatures living in a fallen world. Back to David.

Time passed before a battle ensued between the Philistines and Saul's army. The Philistines had a champion warrior named Goliath. Goliath was taller than every man in that time. We don't know for sure how tall he was, as some ancient manuscripts seem to have exaggerated his height slightly. He was a giant either way when compared to the average person. History shows us that people in that time were, on average, shorter than they are now (an estimated five feet and six inches on average). Goliath was said to be between six feet and nine inches and nine feet tall. Most manuscripts say that he was over nine feet tall (four cubits and a span), while the Dead Sea Scrolls have six feet and nine inches. Either way, he was giant compared to David, who is estimated to be under five feet tall.

> Goliath stood and shouted a taunt across to the Israelites. "Why are you all coming out to fight?" he called. "I am the Philistine champion, but you are only the servants of Saul. Choose one man to come down here and fight me! If he kills me, then we will be your slaves. But if I kill him, you will be our slaves! I defy the armies of Israel today! Send me a man who will fight me!" *(1 Samuel 17:8–10 NLT)*

After this demand, they were terrified about who could possibly beat this giant champion in a head-to-head fight? At this time, David was back helping his father by tending to his sheep. Jesse tells David to take a basket of food to his older brothers, who were part of Saul's army. David left the sheep with another shepherd and made his way to the battleground. The Bible records that this standoff lasted for forty days.

> David left his things with the keeper of supplies and hurried out to the ranks to greet his brothers. As he was talking with them, Goliath, the Philistine champion from Gath, came out from the Philistine ranks. Then David heard him shout his usual taunt to the army of Israel. As soon as the Israelite army saw him, they began to run away in fright. "Have you seen the giant?" the men asked. "He comes out each day to defy Israel. The King has offered a huge reward to anyone who kills him. He will give that man one of his daughters for a wife, and the man's entire fam-

ily will be exempted from paying taxes!" David asked the soldiers standing nearby, "What will a man get for killing this Philistine and ending his defiance of Israel? Who is this pagan Philistine anyway, that he is allowed to defy the armies of the living God?" (*1 Samuel 17:22–26 NLT*)

Hearing this, David went to King Saul and offered to kill Goliath. Saul thought for sure that David would be killed if he went against Goliath and said no. David persisted and explained stories about him killing both lions and bears who were hurting his sheep. This is where David displays his faith in a beautiful way; he tells Saul that God will rescue him from the Philistine just as God rescued him from the lion and the bear. Saul finally agrees and lets David go out to fight. Saul gives David his armor; David puts it on before saying that there is no way he can fight in that because he isn't used to the weight. David then picks up five smooth stones and puts them in his shepherd bag and goes out to face Goliath with only his shepherd staff and an old-school slingshot, which was a piece of leather that you would fold in half around a stone. This sling would be spun rapidly to build up momentum with centrifugal force, and then one of the two halves of the slingshot would be released to project the stone that's held in the middle.

"Am I a dog," he roared at David, "that you come at me with a stick?" And he cursed David by the names of his gods. "Come over here, and I'll give your flesh to the birds and wild animals!" Goliath yelled. David replied to the Philistine, "You come to me with sword, spear, and javelin, but I come to you in the name of the Lord of Heaven's Armies—the God of the armies of Israel, whom you have defied. Today the Lord will conquer you, and I will kill you and cut off your head. And then I will give the dead bodies of your men to the birds and wild animals, and the whole world will know that there is a God in Israel! And everyone assembled here will know that the Lord rescues his people, but not with sword and spear. This is the Lord's battle, and he will give you to us!" *(1 Samuel 17:43–47 NLT)*

This is such an awesome way for David to show his faith and give glory to God before he even fights Goliath. David runs out toward Goliath, pulls out a stone from his bag, puts it into his sling, and propels it toward Goliath as Goliath is moving toward David. The stone sinks into Goliath's skull, causing him to fall down. David runs up, pulls Goliath's sword from its sheath, kills Goliath with his own sword, and hacks off Goliath's head as promised. This impresses Saul immensely.

Could you imagine witnessing this? It would be like a short teenager fighting an Olympic bodybuilder. No one in their right mind would possibly have guessed that David could have won that fight, let alone without being touched at all by this giant. After this, Saul introduced David to his son Jonathan, and they immediately became friends. From this day on, King Saul no longer let David help his father; he wanted David to stay with him. Jonathan and David made a pact with each other to protect each other because they loved each other as themselves.

Anything that David was asked to do by King Saul, David did successfully, which led to David being made a commander over Saul's army. People loved David and began to shout, "Saul has killed his thousands, and David his ten thousands," in 1 Samuel 18:7. This made Saul mad and led to jealousy and even hatred for David; Saul wanted David to die. One day, a spirit came and was messing with Saul, making him go crazy. David came to play his harp as always. During this, Saul tried to kill David with a spear, throwing it at him to try to pin him to the wall. David escaped.

David was sent out into countless battles but always succeeded because God was with him. This scared Saul and made the jealousy grow even more. Saul told David he was ready to give David his oldest daughter, Merab, as a wife, but he first had to prove himself to be worthy by fighting in another battle. Saul thought and hoped that David would die in war so that Saul wouldn't have to kill David himself. David humbled himself after his victory and told Saul that he was not worthy of marrying his daughter, so Saul gave that daughter to a man named Adriel.

Saul's other daughter, Michal, had fallen in love with David, which brought joy to Saul. He told David that he had a second chance to become his son-in-law but would have to go out and fight again in a battle that Saul was certain would kill David. Saul told his soldiers to tell David how much the King liked him and to try to convince David to marry Michal. To this, David replied, "How can a poor man from a humble family afford the bride price for the daughter of a king?" *(1 Samuel 18:23 NLT)*.

Saul's men reported back to Saul, telling him what David said. Saul announced that all he wanted as the bride price was one hundred Philistine foreskins (yes, you read that right). David accepted, went out and killed two hundred Philistines and cut off all of their foreskins, and brought them back to King Saul. After this success and collection of an almost humorous and morbid payment, David married Saul's daughter, Michal.

Saul tried to convince his servants and his son, Jonathan, to kill David. Now if you remember the pact that David and Jonathan made, you'll see why Jonathan, instead, told David about his father's plan. Jonathan then pleaded with his father and begged him not to kill David. Saul promised his son that he would not kill David. So Jonathan told David, and things went back to normal. Well, until one day, the evil spirit came over Saul again. David played his harp again, and just like before, Saul tried to kill David with a spear. The Bible reports that David dodged the spear, and it stuck into the wall behind him, and then David fled and disappeared in the night.

Saul told his men to go watch David's house and to kill him in the morning. Michal heard about this and warned David he needed to escape that night; he did exactly as his wife told him. Saul learned of his daughter's betrayal and became furious with her. She claimed that David threatened to kill her if she didn't help him escape. David fled to find Samuel and told him what had happened, who then took David to live in a place called Ramah.

Saul sent several troops to Ramah to go kill David, but as every troop got there, they all began prophesying. So Saul went himself, and even he began to prophesy, which confused everyone who witnessed the events.

> But on the way to Naioth in Ramah the Spirit of God came even upon Saul, and he, too, began to prophesy all the way to Naioth! He tore off his clothes and lay naked on the ground all day and all night, prophesying in the presence of Samuel. The people who were watching exclaimed, "What? Is even Saul a prophet?" *(1 Samuel 19:23–24 NLT)*

David then ran away and went to find Jonathan. Jonathan denied that his father would try to kill David after swearing that he wouldn't. David explained what happened and even devised a plan to prove that Saul was trying to kill him to prove to Jonathan that he was in danger. During this plan, Saul showed Jonathan how full of hate he was, and Saul even tried to kill Jonathan. So Jonathan went and gave the signal to David that they had agreed upon. Then David said goodbye to Jonathan and escaped from the town.

He went to Gath and lived with King Achish, who was confused by David's arrival. The king heard the stories about David, which made David nervous that King Achish would do something bad to him out of fear or jealousy like Saul. So David acted insane, scratching doors and drooling on himself to make himself seem as though he was not a threat. David then left and hid in a cave where his family would later join him. Then more and more men who were in trouble went to the cave until David was "the captain of about four hundred men" *(1 Samuel 22:2)*.

A prophet named Gad came to David and told him to return to the land of Judah. The news of this spread to King Saul shortly after David had arrived. King Saul started yelling at his men, accusing them of betraying him as his son did and demanding to know why this happened. One of the men told Saul that he saw David meet with priests and collect the sword of Goliath from him. So Saul commanded that all the priests be brought to him and questioned. The priest Ahimelech explained himself.

> "Why have you and the son of Jesse conspired against me?" Saul demanded. "Why did you give him food and a sword? Why have you consulted God for him? Why have you encouraged him to kill me, as he is trying to do this very day?"
>
> "But sir," Ahimelech replied, "Is anyone among all your servants as faithful as David, your son-in-law? Why, he is the captain of your bodyguard and a highly honored member of your household! This was certainly not the first time I had consulted God for him! May the King not accuse me and my family in this matter, for I knew nothing at all of any plot against you." *(1 Samuel 22:13–15 NLT)*

King Saul then ordered his bodyguards to kill the priests, but they refused. Then the king told a man named Doeg to kill them. Doeg did as the king commanded and killed all eighty-five of the priests that were brought before the king. Then he went out and killed the families of those priests, "men and women, children and babies—and all the cattle, donkeys, sheep, and goats" *(1 Samuel 22:19 NLT)*.

Abiathar, one of Ahimelech's sons, was the only survivor and escaped to go tell David what happened. David was deeply saddened by this and told Abiathar to stay with him and told him that he would be protected. David felt personally responsible for all of these deaths, since they were killed because of David getting help from them. Meanwhile, the Philistines were attacking a place called Keilah, stealing their grain. God told David to take his men and go save Keilah. All the men were terrified, but God promised David victory, so they went and defeated the Philistine army. Saul learned of David's new location and ordered his army to go to Keilah and kill David.

> Then David prayed, "O Lord, God of Israel, I have heard that Saul is planning to come and destroy Keilah because I am here. Will the leaders of Keilah betray me to him? And will Saul actually come as I have heard? O Lord, God of Israel, please tell me." And the Lord said, "He will come." Again David asked, "Will the leaders of Keilah betray me and my men to Saul?" And the Lord replied, "Yes, they will betray you." *(1 Samuel 23:10–12 NLT)*

At this time, David now had about six hundred men, and they left Keilah. Saul heard he left, and so he didn't go to Keilah. Instead, Saul hunted and chased after David tirelessly, but God kept David hidden from Saul. Jonathan, however, went and found David. He told David not to give up, to keep strong in his faith, and that soon David will be king instead of Saul. Time passed, and Saul kept hunting and became very close to getting David one day. On that day, he received word that the Philistines were attacking Israel again. King Saul abandoned the search and led his army back to fight the Philistines. After this, the hunt was back on.

One day, Saul decided to get some rest and sleep in a certain cave, unaware that David and his men were hiding in the cave. David's men were telling David to kill Saul while he slept, to take the opportunity to end it all now, but David refused. In fact, David forbade his men from harming Saul either.

> So David restrained his men and did not let them kill Saul. After Saul had left the cave and gone on his way, David came out and shouted after him, "My Lord the King!" And when Saul

looked around, David bowed low before him. Then he shouted to Saul, "Why do you listen to the people who say I am trying to harm you? This very day you can see with your own eyes it isn't true. For the Lord placed you at my mercy back there in the cave. Some of my men told me to kill you, but I spared you. For I said, 'I will never harm the king—he is the Lord's anointed one.' Look, my father, at what I have in my hand. It is a piece of the hem of your robe! I cut it off, but I didn't kill you. This proves that I am not trying to harm you and that I have not sinned against you, even though you have been hunting for me to kill me." *(1 Samuel 24:7–11 NLT)*

Saul cried and realized David was right. He saw that David wasn't actually trying to kill him. Saul asked David to promise not to harm any member of Saul's family when David does eventually become King, and David promised this without hesitation, and then they parted ways. David and his men returned to their stronghold, and Saul and his army returned to their home. Time passed, and Saul gave Michal to a different man, and David found himself a couple of wives.

David got the news that Saul was hunting him again and sent spies out to see if this was true. Finding that it was, David snuck into Saul's camp while Saul and his army slept. David spared his life again, taking the king's spear and water as proof that he could have killed him but didn't. After having a similar conversation as before, Saul understood that he was wrong and asked David to return home with him. David knew that Saul would never stop trying to kill him, so he went to live in Philistine territory under the consent of King Achish. Each day, David and his men would go out and raid Philistine towns, killing every single person that lived there to leave no witnesses. David would tell the king that they raided Israelites, so the king thought that David had for certain burned all of his bridges and would have to live under his control forever.

King Achish was going to battle with King Saul and wanted David at his side in the battle, but the other Philistine men didn't trust David. King Achish told David and his men to return to where they had been living, so they did. When they returned, they found that the Amalekites had raided their town and kidnapped all the women and children, including David's wives. David became fearful of his own men, thinking they would stone him, blaming him for what happened. David prayed and asked God if he should go after the raiders. God said yes and told him to recover everything that was taken. So David went with four hundred of his six hundred men to recover everything and everyone; they were successful.

Meanwhile, the Philistine army was attacking Israel's army and was winning. In this battle, three of Saul's sons, including Jonathan, were killed by the Philistines. Surrounded by Philistines and fearing torture, Saul told his armor-bearer to kill him. This order was refused, so Saul killed himself by falling on his own sword. After seeing this, the armor-bearer also killed himself in the same way. The Philistines found Saul's body. They cut off his head and made mocking displays of his body and head in their pagan temples. Eventually, the Jews heard of this and went to get his body and give it proper respect.

After hearing about Saul's death was the first time the Bible shows David writing a song. He writes a funeral song for Saul. This song expressed respect for the dead as well as David's agony and pain for losing his dearest friend, Jonathan. David asked God if he should move back to Judah, and God said yes. So David and his wives moved back to a town called Hebron. Saul's still living son, Ishbosheth, became king for two years. During this time, most of the citizens remained loyal to David and saw him as king, though he wasn't officially king yet. David's army and Ishbosheth's army went to war; David's army ended up triumphant. Time passed, and Ishbosheth was killed, and his head was presented to David. David didn't order this assassination; in fact, upon hearing this news, he buried Ishboseth's head in his friend Abner's tomb and then had the assassins put to death for murdering Ishobosheth in cold blood as he was lying in his own bed.

After this, all the people chose David to be king. David made a covenant with God and fulfilled the prophecy told by Samuel many years prior. Through many battles to gain all of the land, David remained successful and became more and more powerful as time progressed. David praised God and credited God for their victories in battle. David gathered thirty thousand of the most elite troops in Israel to go get the Ark of the Covenant from Baalah to bring back and put under David's protection. However, upon the way, a man named Uzzah touched the ark, and God immediately killed him for it. This is when David truly started to fear God.

They left the Ark of God with a man named Obed-Edom, whose household was extremely blessed for him holding it. Eventually, David was able to bring it to his city that was named the City of David. After this, David was promised that one of his descendants would be the one who built the temple for the Ark of God (speaking of Solomon). As the Bible states, David reigned over Judah from Hebron for seven and a half years and reigned over all of Israel and Judah from Jerusalem for thirty-three years.

One day, as David was wandering around the roof of his palace, he looked out over the city and saw a beautiful woman taking a bath. David immediately sent out one of his men to find out who she was. It was reported back to him that the woman's name was Bathsheba, the wife of a man named Uriah. Bathsheba was brought to David, who already had multiple wives and mistresses, which led to them having sex. Time passed, and she found out that she was pregnant. She sent word to David to let him know, and this is where things got interesting.

David sent for Uriah to be brought to him. Starting with small talk about the war and how the army was doing, David then told Uriah to go home and relax. David's hope was that Uriah would go home and sleep with his wife, and the baby would then be thought to be Uriah's so that David wouldn't be caught in the adulterous act that he committed. Uriah was an honorable man and refused quietly. He slept all night at the entrance of the palace instead. When David heard about this, he sent for Uriah again to ask why. The answer was along the lines of how unfair it would be for him to go home in comfort to see his wife while his fellow soldiers were fighting and dying.

Before sending him back to the army, David got Uriah drunk and tried again to get Uriah to go home. Even while intoxicated, Uriah refused and again slept at the entrance of the palace. This didn't bode well for David, who desperately didn't want to be caught. So when Uriah was sent back to the army, David sent orders that Uriah was to be put on the front line, where the battle was the most dangerous, to cause Uriah's death. As planned, Uriah died in battle, leaving Bathsheba a widow.

Word was sent to Bathsheba that her husband had died. It was part of the culture to set aside time for a wife to mourn the death of her husband. After this time passed, David sent for Bathsheba to be brought to him, and she became one of his wives, and then she gave birth to a child. God, however, was angry at David for the wicked deed he had done. So to recap that: David saw a woman that he found attractive, had sex with her even though she was already married, got her pregnant, tried to pretend the baby wasn't his by having her husband sleep with her, and then got the husband killed so he could marry Bathsheba and keep the secret about his adultery from everyone else. It's easy to see why God was mad at David.

God sent a prophet named Nathan to yell at David and explain how evil his acts were. David was told that for this deed, the child he bore to Bathsheba would die. Time passed, and Bathsheba became pregnant again, gave birth to a little boy, and David named him Solomon. God loved Solomon and would later choose Solomon to be the successor of David, who would build His temple.

David's life before his reign was full of hardship, and it remained that way throughout the duration of his reign. One of David's sons (Amnon) raped his half sister Tamar, then another one of his sons (Absalom) killed Amnon for raping his sister, and then after being in hiding, Absalom was brought back and forgiven by David. Absalom then led a conspiracy to overthrow his father, at which time David fled for his safety. Taking many of his men and his wives, David left behind some of his mistresses to take care of the palace. Absalom had sex with some of his father's mistresses to further insult his father.

Absalom and his men were hunting for David, trying to find and kill him. During this, Absalom was killed (having three daggers stabbed into his heart). Despite all of this, David was horribly saddened at the news of his son's death and cried violently about it when he heard the news.

> "What about young Absalom?" the King demanded. "Is he all right?" And the Ethiopian replied, "May all of your enemies, my lord the king, both now and in the future, share the fate of that young man!" The King was overcome with emotion. He went up to the room over the gateway and burst into tears. And as he went, he cried, "O my son Absalom! My son, my son Absalom! If only I had died instead of you! O Absalom, my son, my son." *(2 Samuel 18:32–33 NLT)*

After this, David returned to his throne, more depressed than ever before. He punished his mistresses for sleeping with his son in an interesting way; he took care of their needs, fed them, and took care of them in every regard, but he no longer slept with them so they would live like widows until they died. So basically, he withheld sex from the women that he would sleep with when he didn't want to sleep with any of his wives. Interesting, right? They still lived like royalty, but they got no sex from the king.

As David grew older, he got to the point of physical exhaustion where he couldn't fight in battles as well as he used to. In fact, during another battle against the Philistines, David almost died but was saved by a man named Abishai. Second Samuel 22 is the second example given of David's writings. Instead of him expressing his grief, however, David expresses his gratitude for all that God has done for him, praising God and crediting Him with being the source of his strength and the reason for his survival and success through his life. Despite this, David, being a sinful human just like the rest of us, went on to anger God once again.

David took a census of Israel. This action of counting people was forbidden. David's conscience began to burn and sear him with guilt until finally he begged God for his forgiveness. So through the prophet Gad, God gave David three options for how he was to be punished and told David that he must decide his punishment. The options were: three years of famine, three months of fleeing from enemies, or three days of severe plagues. David didn't want his enemies to be the cause of his demise, so he didn't want the fleeing option or the option that would make his soldiers too weak to fight (famine). So for three days, severe illness and sickness came over the people in Israel, killing seventy thousand people. After seventy thousand people died, God told the Angel of Death to stop. When David saw the angel, he cried to God, begging him to kill him and his family instead of the people who were innocent of the decision to sin.

This is not an example that displays God's cruelty, as some would argue; rather, this is a prime example of how just God is and how seriously He views sin. David then was told to build an altar to God to stop the plagues, so he did. Years passed, and David became very old, so old that it was time for him to appoint the next king to replace him. One of David's sons, Adonijah, began declaring that he was the new king. David wasn't aware that this was happening until Bathsheba came to him and told him about it, concerned that David might not keep his promise that their son Solomon would become the next king.

David promised her again and made arrangements for Solomon to be crowned the next king of Israel. David thanked God that he was able to live long enough to see Solomon become the next king. David talked to Solomon, giving him final advice, telling him to always obey God and to keep the commandments of Moses, trying both as a king and a father to give Solomon the best possible parting words before finally dying of old age. David was then buried with his ancestors in the City of David.

Throughout his life, he had an impeccable faith that was displayed on countless occasions. However, he also displayed how he truly felt in his heart—depressed. From arranging the death of Bathsheba's husband so that he could sleep with her despite already having multiple wives and mistresses to literally expressing his sadness verbally and lyrically, David was depressed. The fact that he was vastly wealthier than anyone alive, except for maybe the Pharaoh in Egypt, didn't make a difference to his emotional state. He even had a personal relationship with God and was still depressed. From the time he was a child, fighting off animals that tried to harm his sheep, all the way to his deathbed when he had to solve family drama about who was going to be the next king, David's entire life was difficult and stressful beyond comparison.

The reason we looked so deeply into David's life was as a prerequisite to the following examination into some of the writings of David so you'll have a better understanding of his depression being beaten by his never-ending faith in God. So without further ado, let's dive in and dissect a few of the most notable and beautiful Psalms in scripture, starting with the most popular and most well known—Psalm 23.

> The Lord is my shepherd; I shall not want. He makes me to lie down in green pastures; He leads me beside the still waters. He restores my soul; He leads me in the paths of righteousness for His name's sake. Yea, though I walk through the valley of the shadow of death, I will fear no evil; for You are with me; Your rod and Your staff, they comfort me. You prepare a table before me in the presence of my enemies; You anoint my head with oil; my cup runs over. Surely goodness and mercy shall follow me all the days of my life; and I will dwell in the house of the Lord forever. *(Psalm 23 NKJV)*

Take a moment, read that again if you need to. How beautiful is that? David is expressing that he fears nothing because he trusts God even though he is walking through the "valley of the shadow of death." Whether this is metaphorical or literal, we don't know. Both literal and metaphorical could both be easily argued because of both his depression and because of his countless military encounters. As well as the meaning here being beautiful, his actual poetic nature made this lyrically beautiful as well regardless of what language it is translated into.

> Have mercy on me, O God, according to Your unfailing love; according to Your great compassion blot out my transgressions. Wash away all my iniquity and cleanse me from my sin. For I know my transgressions, and my sin is always before me. Against You, You only, have I sinned and done what is evil in Your sight; so You are right in Your verdict and justified when You judge. Surely I was sinful at birth, sinful from the time my mother conceived me. Yet You desired faithfulness even in the womb; You taught me wisdom in that secret place. Cleanse me with hyssop, and I will be clean; wash me, and I will be whiter than snow. Let me hear joy and gladness; let the bones You have crushed rejoice. Hide Your face from my sins and blot out all my iniquity. Create in me a pure heart, O God, and renew a steadfast spirit within me. Do not cast me from Your presence or take Your Holy Spirit from me. Restore to me the joy of your salvation and grant me a willing spirit, to sustain me. Then I will teach transgressors Your ways, so that sinners will turn back to You. Deliver me from the guilt of bloodshed, O God, You who are God my Savior, and my tongue will sing of Your righteousness. Open my lips, Lord, and my mouth will declare Your praise. You do not delight in sacrifice, or I would bring it; You do not take pleasure in burnt offerings. My sacrifice, O God, is a broken spirit; a broken and contrite heart You, God, will not despise. May it please You to prosper Zion, to

build up the walls of Jerusalem. Then You will
delight in the sacrifices of the righteous, in burnt
offerings offered whole; then bulls will be offered
on Your altar. *(Psalm 51 NIV)*

Side notes written into various Bibles state that this was written
by David right after being approached by the prophet Nathan in
regard to his various sins involving Bathsheba and her first husband.
There are a few lines in this Psalm that hit me every time I hear or
read it, and it's been that way since the very first time I read them.
The very first line expresses the entire premise of this beautiful and
poetic plea for God's forgiveness: "Have mercy on me, O God." Can
that possibly be worded in any other way to show how direct and
simplistic his youth-like prayer is? He knows he's done wrong as he
confesses, "Against You, You only, have I sinned and done what is evil
in Your sight," before continuing to say, "Create in me a pure heart,
O God, and renew a steadfast spirit within me. Do not cast me from
Your presence or take Your Holy Spirit from me."

This is so beautiful. This is David repenting. If you will recall,
back to step 7, we talked about how crucial repentance is and how it
is being born again when God creates a pure heart in you in place of
your sinful, deceiving heart. David admits his sinful nature and begs
for God's forgiveness and mercy. Finally, David expresses his depression as plainly as possible in this Psalm in verse 17: "My sacrifice, O
God, is a broken spirit; a broken and contrite heart You, God, will
not despise." His sacrifice to God wasn't burnt offerings or the sacrifice of animals; it was his broken spirit, his broken heart. He was stat-
ing here that he was giving his life to God and sacrificing himself to
God. This is similar to Paul's testimony when he states in Galatians
2:20 that he has been crucified with Christ, so it is no longer Paul
that lives but rather Christ that lives in him.

Give thanks to the Lord, for he is good;
his love endures forever. Let Israel say: "His love
endures forever." Let the house of Aaron say:
"His love endures forever." Let those who fear the

Lord say: "His love endures forever." When hard pressed, I cried to the Lord; he brought me into a spacious place. The Lord is with me; I will not be afraid. What can mere mortals do to me? The Lord is with me; he is my helper. I look in triumph on my enemies. It is better to take refuge in the Lord than to trust in humans. It is better to take refuge in the Lord than to trust in princes. All the nations surrounded me, but in the name of the Lord I cut them down. They surrounded me on every side, but in the name of the Lord I cut them down. They swarmed around me like bees, but they were consumed as quickly as burning thorns; in the name of the Lord I cut them down. I was pushed back and about to fall, but the Lord helped me. The Lord is my strength and my defense; he has become my salvation. Shouts of joy and victory resound in the tents of the righteous: "The Lord's right hand has done mighty things! The Lord's right hand is lifted high; the Lord's right hand has done mighty things!" I will not die but live, and will proclaim what the Lord has done. The Lord has chastened me severely, but he has not given me over to death. Open for me the gates of the righteous; I will enter and give thanks to the Lord. This is the gate of the Lord through which the righteous may enter. I will give you thanks, for you answered me; you have become my salvation. The stone the builders rejected has become the cornerstone; the Lord has done this, and it is marvelous in our eyes. The Lord has done it this very day; let us rejoice today and be glad. Lord, save us! Lord, grant us success! Blessed is he who comes in the name of the Lord. From the house of the Lord we bless you. The Lord is God, and he has made his light shine on us. With boughs in hand, join in the festal procession up to the horns of the altar. You are my God, and I will praise you; you are my God, and I will exalt you. Give thanks to the Lord, for he is good; his love endures forever. *(Psalm 118 NIV)*

If you read the introduction to this book, you should have been able to guess that Psalm 118 would have been one of the psalms discussed. This one is so beautiful and is the chapter in the Bible that I hold dearest to my heart. "When hard-pressed, I cried to the Lord; he brought me into a spacious place," would be the first of the verses in this section that I want to touch on. God answering prayers is one of the most beautiful gifts that we can experience in this world. Just to know that God hears us and getting that confirmation of Him listening by the fulfillment of our prayers is so wonderful and, in and of itself, miraculous.

"It is better to take refuge in the Lord than to trust in humans. It is better to take refuge in the Lord than to trust in princes." Following the close, after verse 5, we find these beautiful verses that tell us not to trust anyone except God. This is beautiful and saddening at the same time. As humans, we want to have hope that people are good and that there are just some bad apples. Reality hits deep when we find that no one is good except for God *(Mark 10:18)*, which is why the only one we can truly depend on is God. Now I'm not telling you not to trust anyone for any reason, ever. I'm telling you to understand that humans can and will break your trust. However, God will never break your trust. It is impossible for God to lie *(Hebrews 6:18)*, and so God can never break your trust under any circumstance.

"I was pushed back and about to fall, but the Lord helped me. The Lord is my strength and my defense; He has become my salvation." Just read that again real quick. Here, the expression is made that God has helped him. Many people have this very inaccurate image of God in their mind (which is idolatry, to imagine God differently than how he revealed himself to us through scripture) in which God is a deist. This means that God is like a clockmaker, where he winds up the clock and just lets it go without interacting with His creation. This is obviously not an accurate description of the God of the Bible, who is constantly intervening and helping us as expressed here. God is not an inactive creator; He is active in our lives, yet He allows us to make mistakes on our own so that we can learn the lessons He wants us to learn.

This is made even more amazing by the word here for "salvation," in Hebrew יְשׁוּעָה, which transliterated is *yᵉšû ʿâ*. This word literally means "salvation by God.' This word is pronounced "Yesh-oo'-aw," which those of you with some Bible knowledge will know as the Hebrew pronunciation of Jesus's name. This means that this verse would be read by ancient Jews as, "I was pushed back and about to fall, but the Lord helped me. The Lord is my strength and my defense; he has become my Jesus."

This is so cool and very comforting for those like me who have felt abandoned and alone in the world with no options left. It's a soothing and reassuring thing to know that God is always there, and He doesn't abandon us, and He revealed the name that He would take when He became incarnate.

What we would learn from this is that writing is going to help us. Writing is a very therapeutic way to express your thoughts and emotions in a very private and healthy way. A lot of people will refuse to try writing because they say they don't know what to write about. So let me help you with that right now. First, I'm going to tell you the style that I recommend writing in, and then I'm going to prompt you with questions that I want you to answer. Remember, you're not writing for anyone except for yourself, so feel free to destroy what you write when you're done, but be completely honest in what you write; that way, it is a true venting expression of your thoughts and feelings.

The style that I would recommend for you, to begin with, is a basic rhyming poem or song. There have been multiple studies done that have shown the action of rhyming words actually causes the release of endorphins in your brain. This is to say, rhyming what you write will not only make the process more entertaining for you but also will be more effective at making you feel better while venting.

The rhyme scheme that you make doesn't have to be good, so don't worry about that. You'll be surprised, however, at how fast your skills will improve in terms of your vocabulary and linguistic knowledge. I have written well over one thousand songs/poems over the years, all based around this rhyming concept, and it works.

When rhyming, there are a few different versions of rhyming: imperfect and perfect. The imperfect rhyme schemes are better for the creative aspects of this because they will broaden your options as well as increase your imaginative abilities. A perfect rhyme consists of words that sound close to identical but not identical. Imperfect rhymes focus primarily on the sound of the vowel, putting less emphasis on the consonance. Synonyms would be good examples of perfect rhymes such as *night* and *knight*, but above this, you could incorporate words that are not identical in pronunciation (*bright, sight, site, light, fight, write, right*, etc.). Imperfect rhymes that focus more on the vowel contained in each syllable with less emphasis on the consonance will be exemplified by words like *got no, stop go, shot low, pop so, macho, taco*, etc.

When I'd feel sad, lonely, suicidal, depressed, anxious, angry, or any other negative emotion, I'd write. I'd write about the day, my thoughts, how I'm feeling physically, about my fears, about my hopes, and anything that could come into my mind. I've written songs about girlfriends before and after the end of the relationship, I've written poems about God, and the first thing I did the day my grandfather died was—you guessed it—write. Again, feel free to delete and/or destroy what you write so no one else ever reads it if you don't want it to be read, though I'd recommend keeping them so you can go back through and read what you have written.

Most of the writing I've done, I still have saved on my password-protected smartphone so that I can look back at what I was feeling, how my writing style has altered, how my emotional and mental states have improved, and much more. It's also therapeutic to read that which you wrote long ago to see how life has altered for you. Reading stuff that I wrote ten years ago blows my mind, not only on how much I've grown mentally but also how differently I look at the world in comparison.

In Jordan Peterson's book, *Beyond Order*, rule 9 states that you should write down your worst memories in as much detail as possible. Prior to reading his book and prior to writing this book, I wrote an entire novel about the dream that I had years ago that really began the amplification of my depression. The dream was horrendous and led to a wonderful horror story, which, as of writing this, I have yet to publish. The point is, he's correct in this exercise. It really does help because it allows you to step out of your own mind and look at it from an outside perspective. So while I found that writing songs and poems are the most effective for me, there is a chance that writing in the way Dr. Peterson suggests could be more effective for you.

As for the prompts, these are a few questions that I want you to answer when you initially begin your literary journey into sanity:

1. How are you feeling right now mentally? Are you mentally tired, happy, stressed, scared, sad, nervous, anxious, excited, disappointed, distraught, mad, etc.?

2. What's making you feel that way? Did something happen today? Did you have a bad dream? Is some event coming up later this week or month that you are or are not looking forward to? Describe exactly what's making you feel the way that you're feeling. If it's one of those days that you don't know what's making you feel the way you're feeling, explain lyrically that you don't know why you're feeling that way. Tell the story about the cause.

3. What could or should make you feel better than you're feeling right now? Is there a solution to your current problem? If so, can you achieve that solution? If you can, write out your plan of attack for solving the issue. If there is not a known solution for your problem, write a prayer to God for help in finding that solution. Don't pray for a solution, pray for the ability to find the solution. If your initial problem is missing a loved one who has passed away, pray for comfort and relief from your pain.

That's it—start writing based on that. It could start out as simplistic or right off the bat, and then you can try to incorporate metaphors and imagery into the writing to add to the poetry of the piece. Feel free to use cliche imagery at first to get your mind thinking in that way (dark skies, bad weather, etc.). To end this chapter, I'm going to give you a simplistic example of what this style of writing could look like. This is a short poem that I wrote as a prayer to God.

## Better Now

Back in the day, I truly wanted suicide,
Focusing on women, but now I focus on You and I.
*It was inevitable*, I thought, *that every human dies.*
    *So why prolong my pain with days that are*
    *scrutinized?*
I was just unhappy and had to see through the
    pride,
Paul said we're predestined, so You decide
Who survives this ruthless life,
Show me Your will, God, I'll move aside.

This is my truest side that I'm revealing to You,
It's like I'm appealing to the ceiling but I'm griev-
    ing to who,
To You, the God of wisdom, peace, and clarity.
I thank You in this moment for blessing me with
    therapy,
I was burying so carefully the scary things that
    stare so deep
Into my soul, but I dug them up so You could
    share with me
The lessons of my past and how You'd bear with
    me.
Then You gifted me with grace because You
    apparently cared for me,
I thank You, God, for sparing me,

It's Your strength that carries me.
I deserve death, You paid the debt; that seems
      unfair to me,
A love like Yours is a rarity,
You provided grace to my heart's charity,
When my soul could barely breathe, You've been
      there for me,
God, I thank You…with sincerity.

Amen.

# STEP 9

# Physical Health Is Mental Health

> Do you not know that your bodies are temples of the Holy Spirit, who is in you, whom you have received from God? You are not your own; you were bought at a price. Therefore honor God with your bodies. *(1 Corinthians 6:19–20 NIV)*

Many who hear this verse think that it refers to abstaining from sin, specifically sexual sin; while this is correct, it also involves you understanding that God not only made you but died to keep you and, therefore, is not only about sexual sin. Our bodies are gifts that we must cherish and care for. The vast majority of people who find themselves living in depression do the exact opposite of taking care of themselves. They turn to drugs, alcohol abuse, or develop eating disorders (which can be just as bad and even worse than the prior). All of these are horrible because it's hurting your physical health, which damages your mental health.

In fact, I would argue that the act of not taking care of yourself, getting fat, eating junk, and not working out is just as sinful as anything else. For example, in the story of Sodom and Gomorrah, the people there were all idolatrous, homosexual, rapists, and murderers. The Bible says there wasn't a single innocent person there, so God ordered the Angel of Death to destroy it and kill everyone there. Yet if we look at Ezekiel, we can see that it compares being selfish and gluttonous with the sins of Sodom.

> Now this was the sin of your sister Sodom: She and her daughters were arrogant, overfed and unconcerned; they did not help the poor and needy. *(Ezekiel 16:49 NIV)*

Our bodies are amazing creations that are high-functioning machines. Just like any other type of machine, we must take care of it, especially since our bodies are so precious and so valuable. Every part of your body is connected to every other part of your body. This includes your muscles and your brain. It's been scientifically proven time and time again that those who stay active and exercise on a regular basis handle stress much better, are overall happier, and get sick less often.

Everyone will try to make excuses as to why they should be lazy and avoid taking care of themselves, so let me do my best to explain why none of your excuses matter. Some people say they hurt too much to work out. I have torn ligaments in both of my shoulders from an old injury that occurred when I was sixteen. At seventeen, I tore my psoas muscle while working. I've had shin splints, plantar fasciitis, carpal tunnel, tennis and golfer elbow, headaches from chronic inflammatory conditions as a result of getting minor heat stroke (also when I was sixteen), back pain like most have never experienced, among many other injuries. The point is, despite the pain I'm in on a regular basis, I make it a goal to work out every single day, and you know what? My body hurts significantly less when I work out.

Some people say they don't have time to work out. Well, I currently own and operate two small businesses at the same time that I am writing this book and another book that is also Bible-based but on a much different subject. I have little free time, but I make myself work out for at least thirty minutes a day to keep myself healthy and active. My point with these arguments is not to say that my life is busier than yours or that my pain is worse than yours; my point is that you can make it work, and you need to make it work if you want to be happier and healthier.

So how should you do this? Well, start with getting a goal in mind. Do you want to lose weight? Do you want to get stronger? Do you want to get fit? Do you want to increase your endurance? Each goal is going to have a different journey, and all will end with better mental health, so let's talk about each of them.

Starting with losing weight as a goal, since it is one of the most common goals in the realm of physical health, there are going to be a few things to tackle. The first is going to be the food you eat, not just the type but the frequency as well. This aspect of health is going to vary the most based on the kind of goal that you're establishing, but it will have one common theme throughout: eat less sugar. There are two types of sugar that we consume on a daily basis, which are complex sugars (polysaccharides) and simple sugars (monosaccharides). Simple sugars are overprocessed sugars that break down in your body at a very fast pace. This type of sugar is the bad sugar that's found in foods like candy and soda. Complex sugars are the unprocessed/natural sugars that break down slower in your body and thus are better for you, as they provide a more genuine form of energy. This type of sugar is found in foods like fruits and vegetables.

The complex (good) sugars are not what I'm telling you to avoid; it's the bad sugar that you should avoid. Many studies have shown a direct correlation between the amount of sugar consumed and the level of depression that an individual experiences. Sugar, just like nicotine or any other drug, boosts your dopamine levels to a level that cannot be reached naturally. This results in an addiction to the substance that is delivering those happy chemicals to your brain. Every soda you drink, candy bar you eat, cigarette you smoke, or line of cocaine you snort is like a tiny mailman who delivers a package of temporary joy to the brain. Once you use up all the joy, your mind craves more. It becomes your only mission to get more of it. This sounds far-fetched to correlate cocaine to sugar, but it's not.

Both of those innocent-looking white powders cause severe damage to your body and make your brain think it will die if it doesn't get more. When was the last time you ate something sugary? A week ago? A day ago? A few hours ago? How long will it be until you get a craving for more sugar? Have you ever had a craving for something sweet so intensely that you actually started to get frustrated when you couldn't have it at the time? That is addiction. That is your brain needing a foreign substance to feel happy. Then after you get your fix, it goes away, but soon you crave more.

Breaking that addiction is going to be difficult, but it will also be beneficial. Just by quitting sugar, you're immediately going to start to lose some weight. Combine that with getting more active, and you'll be surprised at how fast you start to lose it. Reducing the amount of food you eat is also going to be crucial. A good and simple rule of thumb is this: to lose weight, eat fewer calories than you burn. Sounds simple, right? It is.

Reducing sugar and quantity will be huge, but we also want to look at how often we are eating. Are you eating three meals a day and having snacks in between? Stop snacking or skip a meal. You can find entire books on intermittent fasting, which is why we are only going to briefly cover the concept here. It's quite simple, though. The most common form of intermittent fasting is the 8/16-hour division. This is where you get eight hours to eat and sixteen hours to starve (or fast, if you prefer the nicer-sounding word). The easiest way to schedule your day around this would be to skip breakfast. If you wait until noon to start eating and don't eat past 8:00 p.m., then you will be sleeping for about eight hours of that starvation period.

The point of intermittent fasting is quite interesting. While it varies from person to person, studies have shown that the average body will enter into what's called ketosis after approximately twelve hours of fasting. Ketosis is where your body (in simple terms) stops using sugar for energy and starts burning fat for energy instead. This is wonderfully beneficial for those who want to lose weight because it means you will be burning fat passively. Combining this with eating healthy and working out, you will start seeing results in the first week.

You could take this a step further and try eating in a certain way, like the keto diet, for example. While there are many different versions of the same diet, the big rule of thumb is to stop eating carbs. Eat vegetables and meat but be sure that you don't consume more than fifty grams of carbs per day, and your body will remain in ketosis until you break the diet. Adding this to your arsenal of health is going to give you a fighting advantage in your quest to get healthier.

This specific example of doing an 8/16-hour fast is best for those who work a nine-to-five job and is just that, an example. You can mix up any of the concepts you'd like and tailor it to fit your life and your schedule. The main thing to take from this is to clean up your diet and eat fewer calories than you burn. Also, remember that everyone is different, so you might have to eat differently than some, and you may have to work harder than some. Regardless, everyone can lose weight and get into amazing shape. The next part of this is the fun part that you will hate until you love it—working out.

This aspect of working out is going to be applied to all goals listed previously in this step, especially this piece right here: work out every day. That's right, every single day, I want you to work out. Is there a day that you really don't feel like it? Push through that fog, make yourself do it even if it's only a small workout. When trying to burn more calories than you eat, the best type of workout will be a high-intensity cardio workout of some kind. Whether this is running, jogging, biking, swimming, dancing, competitive fighting, free running, or even speed walking, the goal is to get your heart beating fast and burning through calories.

If you're not sweating, you need to push harder. In combination with cardio, you also need to start doing some weightlifting. For the goal of losing weight, getting fit, or recovering from injuries, you don't want to be lifting heavyweight. The best way to achieve these goals is to lift lighter weight at a much higher scale. For example, if you are going to do bicep curls, which do you think will burn more calories and teach your muscles how to properly contract again—lifting sixty pounds ten times or lifting ten pounds sixty times? It's going to be the lighter weight and higher repetitions.

Not only is this going to retrain your muscles on how to properly contract, but it will also turn every workout you're doing into more cardio/endurance training. Now say, you're already in pretty decent shape but you want to bulk up and increase the size of your muscles, you're going to want to do both. Starting with the lightweight and high reps and then gradually increase the weight (which will naturally reduce the reps). The heavier weight and fewer reps will cause larger microtears in the fascia of the muscle tissue, which will result in more soreness, longer recovery time, and faster size development than the lighter weight option. A good mixture of both of these methods would be beneficial at any level, though; just give more focus on the one that lines up with your goal.

The most important part of this is when you work out, not in terms of morning or night—that is your choice based on you as an individual. What I'm talking about is working out when the bad thoughts come. When I was quitting nicotine, I was extremely short-tempered for months. When I got mad and was craving nicotine, I made myself do push-ups no matter where I was. When I feel lonely, I go running. When I feel sad, I lift weights. Fortunately for me, I used to feel all these emotions at once and could therefore knock out a good hour at the gym in one cycle.

As you do positive habitual activities like these, you're going to stop viewing them negatively and will start to view them in a positive light. Some people absolutely hate working out. If that's you, then you need to start working out immediately. It starts off as being a hassle and is one of the worst things you can do until you start to enjoy it and look forward to it every day. The job I currently have is very physically demanding, so after a full day of work, I sometimes dread going to the gym in the evening. Regardless, I make myself go, and I'm always happy that I did. I'll feel exhausted and completely debilitated, but mentally I'll feel better because I accomplished the daily goal, the daily task, the daily healthy vice that edged me closer to the long-term fitness goal I set for myself.

> Whoever is patient has great understanding,
> but one who is quick-tempered displays folly.
> *(Proverbs 14:29 NIV)*

The next part of this is going to be patience. Trying to lose weight or put on weight doesn't matter for this point: do not weigh yourself daily. Today, weigh yourself naked, write down the weight, and forget about it. Start eating healthy, working out, and don't weigh yourself for two weeks. After the two-week mark, you can start weighing yourself on a weekly basis. Why? Well, this is a slow process; you do not lose a lot overnight just like you didn't gain it overnight. Therefore, the slow progression could be discouraging and make you want to give up because you're not seeing the results as fast as you want.

Patience is going to be key for almost every step that we have covered. Reading the Bible takes time, getting healthy takes time, achieving goals takes time, waiting for prayers to be answered takes time, reaching others with the gospel takes time...it takes time to beat depression.

> Therefore, as God's chosen people, holy and dearly loved, clothe yourselves with compassion, kindness, humility, gentleness and patience. *(Colossians 3:12 NIV)*

So how can your mental health increase with your physical health? Your body and your brain are connected. This sounds like a no-brainer, and it kind of is. Your brain is fully aware of absolutely everything going on in your body on both a conscious and a subconscious level. We are such amazing creations that work in ways that we may never fully understand; however, what we do understand is that our brain is a reflection of our bodies and vice versa. If our physical health is suffering, it's often a reflection of our mental health.

Suppose you invest time into learning about body language, psychology, sociology, as well as anatomy and physiology. In that case, you will start to see these things in others and in yourself, which give you clues as to what one might be feeling mentally based on what they are presenting physically—for example, eyes. When I'm in public, I am hypervigilant of other people and pay close attention to their eyes. Are they discolored? Makeup smeared? What are they looking at? Are they avoiding eye contact? Do they have "shifty eyes" or even a blank stare?

I look for this stuff for multiple reasons, from a defensive/protective point of view all the way to a caring point of view. If someone looks threatening, I want to be aware of that as soon as possible so the chance of survival for myself and those around me can increase. In some cases, I've seen people who look at their feet constantly, only looking up briefly to confirm their insecurities to see if anyone is looking at them judgmentally. Typically, if someone is looking down, slouching, and avoiding eye contact with others, there's usually something going on. It could be as minor as a bad day, or it could be a sign of a deeper issue like depression.

If I see these people, I try to go out of my way to do something nice for them. It could be as simple as complimenting someone's shoes or even striking up a conversation by making a stupid joke. I know it sounds kind of weird, especially if you're introverted like me, to go talk to a random person who doesn't seem like they want to talk. When I think that way, though, I just think back to the previous steps, and I actively choose to love my neighbor. I've talked to people who looked very depressed. They were shy and didn't want to talk and felt nervous, but little things go a long way.

As a specific example, I was in a restaurant, getting food to take home. While waiting in line, I noticed the woman behind me in line was presenting these signs that told me she was having a bad day. She avoided eye contact with people, even the server she was speaking with, while at the same time seeming to struggle with keeping her eyes open. She kept her head downturned and was performing multiple soothing gestures back-to-back, moving her arms between hugging herself and palpating her suprasternal notch, as well as stroking the back of one of her hands with the other. The poor woman seemed quite frantic. I have no idea what happened to her that day, let alone that week, but a little goes a long way. When I got to the register, I discreetly told the cashier that I wanted to pay for the woman's food. So the cashier rang me up, and I went on my way. When I got outside the restaurant and blended into the dark cover of night, I looked back inside just in time to see the woman begin to tear up lightly in shock as she started looking around for the man who paid for her food.

Something as small as buying a $7 burrito for a stranger made the woman's day significantly better. Was it because she got free food? Of course not. It's because she saw that a random person cared enough about her to do something nice. In other situations that I've seen people in this kind of mood, I'll compliment them on something and watch their facial expressions change instantly from empty to full of joy.

"Oh, dude, I like your shoes."

"Huh?" they'd say back as they wake up from their depressing daydreaming.

"Your shoes, they look sweet. I've been looking to get new ones, mine are getting worn out. Do you like yours?" I'd press.

"Yeah, I love them! Super comfy and great arch support," they'd say as they start to open up a little. You can see the small amount of attention you give to them; it starts to show them that someone cares. Sometimes that's all it takes.

Just don't be creepy with your compliments! That's important! Telling someone a compliment based on affirming a choice they made is much better than complimenting someone on their physical appearance. For example, complimenting the way a woman styled her hair is a lot better than complimenting how her face looks. See? Even that sounds creepy.

So why did I go onto this little tangent? To remind you to love your neighbor while also telling you one way that your mental health becomes physically visible. Though these examples dwell mostly on a person's mood, other physical signs will reveal deeper issues in people's minds. When someone is severely overweight, it shows the outside world one simple thing: you hate yourself. I know it sounds harsh, and if you're reading this and you are overweight, you might want to argue that point, so let me explain.

Someone who is severely overweight is someone who has basically made it a point in life to neglect caring for themselves. Eating garbage food and never working out is hating yourself. If you raised a child and only fed them bad food, that would be abuse. If you never let them be active, that would be abuse. If you don't treat yourself how you should treat a child that you're raising in terms of caring for the child and watching out for their health and safety, then you are hating yourself.

Loving ourselves isn't the primary goal; rather, it's loving God and caring for his creation. If you were to imagine your body to be a car, you might be able to understand this concept more clearly. In order for a car to work after it is made, it must be maintained and cared for. Fuel must be put into the vehicle but not just any fuel; it has to be the right kind for your specific vehicle. Occasionally, parts of the vehicle will have issues, and those issues will have to be addressed in order to function properly. Some of these forms of maintenance can be done by yourself, while others will require someone else to do it for you. Most people can change their own oil, but most people can't fix their own alignment. So let the oil represent supplements such as vitamins while the alignment will represent our body's structural integrity.

Throughout all of the injuries that I have experienced in my life, I've found that getting bodywork is essential to physical health, not only when hurting but also when trying to increase your overall wellness. Things like massage therapy and chiropractic care are hugely important for taking care of your body. The most important of these is massage. Not some Swedish tickle massage but rather a real structural/injury massage to properly get the muscles working again. If you are trying to get in shape but you aren't taking care of your muscles to make sure they can contract fully and properly, you are going to struggle to achieve the results that you're looking for.

Taking care of your physical health is truly going to make a world of difference when it comes to your mental health. When it comes to working out being beneficial, it isn't just the results of the workout that will help you but also the actual act of working out itself. Our society wants to pretend that humans are no longer humans, that we no longer possess a physical need to vent or release built-up aggression—this is a fallacy. We physically must release this anger and aggression that builds in us. One of the healthiest ways to do that is by lifting weights, running, skateboarding, skiing, or even competing in sports. These are workouts that allow us to safely release that stress and rage in healthy ways.

As we become more physically active, we will find that our minds are becoming less haunted by rage. Most people with anger problems, aside from those experiencing anger as a side effect of something like nicotine withdrawals, will also be battling with depression and will be people who do not take the time to exercise on a regular basis. "Well, I have an active job, so that's my workout," is something that is commonly said by people that meet this psychological profile. Though the job is physically demanding, and they do gain strength from it, these people rarely actually do specific and targeted workouts outside of work.

The workouts they are doing at their job aren't being done for the purpose of getting stronger or getting in shape; they are being done for the purpose of accomplishing the job, even if the job is something that person scornfully despises. If this is the case, the physical exertion at the job is only going to be fueling the fire even more, which will result in not only more anger but also resentment for the job and those around you—those you work with and those you work for.

Now when referring to those you work for, I'm not talking about the company that you are employed by. While that is a possible outcome as well, I'm talking about the ones you work to provide for, like your spouse, your kids, yourself. This isn't saying to quit your job and get another one (while in some cases that may be what's best), but this is emphasizing the importance of you working out to physically express that rage that builds inside all of us. There are multiple reasons for the increase in public fits of violence in this world. In many cases, these mass murderers never found a way to vent their rage and instead let it build until it erupted and they snapped. A reason above this is that they never knew God. Those who truly know God are born again and would never harm the innocent people around us. Those who are born again still struggle with anger and sin, but we find healthy ways to vent the anger so that we do not experience such an explosion of violence.

This takes us back to loving our neighbors as ourselves. To do this, we must first be taking care of ourselves so that we can physically and mentally take care of others. Be it in providing for our family financially or in physically taking the burdens of others upon ourselves, we must ensure we are capable of helping others and, therefore, loving them. Jesus taught us many things. He commanded us to do many things as well. However, the most important teaching He shared with us had nothing to do with our lives.

Jesus's most important and most impactful message to all of mankind was how to be saved, how to truly trust and accept Christ. We have this false understanding of God in the world that stems from Hollywood, televangelist preachers who do not teach the biblical Gospel, and books written by people who claim to be Christian and then blaspheme God by trying to give Him manlike traits and characteristics. So to help with your mental health, I think it would be very beneficial to end this step by explaining who God is according to the Bible.

I've talked with many people about God and the Gospel, and one of the biggest things I hear is people telling me that they are saved because God is forgiving. This is an unfortunate misconception about God that a lot of people who think they are Christians have been led to believe. God is good; therefore, God is a just God who upholds justice. If He forgave everyone of everything that they have done, then He wouldn't be just and upright. God must uphold his law. We as humans desire to see punishment for those who do evil because we are made in God's image.

Take, for example, a man who rapes and murders multiple people. We desperately want that man to be punished. We want justice to be done. God wants justice too. Our standard of justice is different from God's standard of justice. God views those who have told a single lie to be worthy of death and, therefore, Hell *(Revelation 21:8)*. Those who have ever stolen something (even if it's as minor as illegally downloading a song off the internet), those who have ever cheated, those who have ever blasphemed His name, those who have ever coveted, dishonored their parents, prayed to anything or anyone besides God, etc.—God views them the same as we could view a murderer.

Sin is so serious in God's eyes that He will punish us for eternity for sinning. God is a just and righteous God. However, God is also a very merciful God. Jesus didn't die for no reason. Jesus died to give us a way to escape Hell, to escape God's wrath, to be free from the curse that accompanies sin. Jesus died in our place. The punishment must be served, but fortunately for us, Jesus took that punishment on our behalf. So does God forgive sins? Yes, but only the sins of those who put their soul's salvation solely in the hands of Jesus Christ, our Lord.

Repent and trust in Christ. That is how you obtain God's mercy. That is how you escape Hell. That is how you will be forgiven. That is how you will inherit eternal life. That is how (the only way how) we can be saved. We are born as the enemy of God; our carnal minds hate our creator. God loved his enemy so much that He gave us a way to escape the fates that we deserve. God's grace is the only source of hope and salvation in this life and our eternity after.

So to achieve that mental health, it is good and healthy to understand that we do not deserve God's mercy, we are entitled to nothing, and we all deserve eternal punishment. Seems dark, right? Not when you look at it biblically. That means God loves you so much that He died so that you may live. So while we deserve Hell, God loved us and saved those who trust in Christ from that eternal agony and separation from God.

Even if you feel that no one loves you, when you feel alone and hopeless, remember that God literally came to earth and died while He was specifically thinking about you. He is all-knowing, all-powerful, and knows the entire life of every single person that has ever lived or will ever live. He didn't just die for some of your sins; He died for all of your sins, all of my sins, and every sin that has ever been and will ever be committed by those who trust fully in Jesus Christ as our savior.

> For by one sacrifice he has made perfect forever those who are being made holy. *(Hebrews 10:14 NIV)*

# EPILOGUE

I wouldn't make any of these suggestions to you if they didn't work for me. I have been miserable a large portion of my life, which is no one's fault but my own. I have allowed myself to be the victim of my own circumstances. To live life focusing on tragic events as if those are actually bad events. While we view them as bad, we must trust that they have a purpose. So I'd like to share a few more intimate and specific details with you about my experiences to show you the good that came from the bad.

First and perhaps the most apparent is that the damage that I have mentally acquired over the years is the sole reason I'm writing this book. Step 8 wasn't just good advice; it was a learned skill that provided me with clarity as well as therapy. If you will recall, at the very beginning of this book, I was talking about the number 118. I mentioned a rapper whose birthday was on 11-8. In an interview, this rapper was asked if writing his songs was therapeutic for him. I can't remember his exact quote, but he affirmed that was his only therapy.

So I pondered on the idea and thought, *If he can do it, why can't I? If it helps him, why not me?* From then on, I began writing songs. I was in high school, and it was the beginning of my senior year. The teachers at my school were allowed to request having students, that they had previously taught, return to their class for the following semester. This was the only time a teacher ever liked me, let alone put me in the top three students he wanted to have again. I was in his class for three total semesters, and to this day, I hold more respect for that man than all of my other teachers combined.

The first day of his class that year, he asked, "How was every-one's summer? Did anyone write any poetry?" Very sarcastically, I responded by making some joke about how no one has written poetry since the late nineteenth century. I got a few laughs and was then stunned when he stood perfectly still, looked me straight in the eye, and started rapping. Not just rapping but rapping a very well-written song that utilizes the same type of rhyming sequencing that I recommended back in step 8.

I sat back and put my hands up in defeat. This middle-aged English teacher recited lines from one of the most popular rap songs ever released to show me what I had never considered before: songs are poems, rap is poetry. This caught my attention for his class. It was at that moment that I realized, yeah, I guess I wrote around one hundred poems that summer. I was seventeen at the time, and about a year and a half had passed since I initially got injured (both physi-cally and mentally).

The bad stuff that I experienced gave me a story to tell, a subject to write about, and a rage that I needed to vent. Now I had an outlet for that venting. At this time, I was still what I would consider to be an atheist, though as Dr. Jordan B. Peterson stated it, "there are no atheists, only people who know and don't know what god they serve."

The second commandment in the Bible is one that we briefly covered in step 3. This commandment forbids idolatry, which is cre-ating a fake god to worship or worshiping a being besides the one true God. Be it that you are attempting to give God human characteristics or trying to imagine Him in any way other than how He has revealed Himself to us in scripture, it's idolatry and, therefore, a false god that you have created in your mind. In this way, we can see that some peo-ple will hold a god of sorts at the center of their life. When speaking to a rich man, Jesus was asked how to enter heaven. Jesus tests him by the commandments, and when the man says that he has done good and lived by the Ten Commandments, Jesus tells him to give away his money and join him. The man got sad and walked away.

The reason for this was that the rich man's god was actually his money, and Jesus knew this. He loved his money more than he loved God and, therefore, violated the first and second commandments.

Jesus then said in Matthew 19:24 (NIV), "Again I tell you, it is easier for a camel to go through the eye of a needle than for someone who is rich to enter the kingdom of God." The reason it's so hard for a rich person to enter heaven isn't because they are rich; it's because they are too comfortable. They are rich and they love their money more than they love the God who blessed them with it. They love the comfort in their lives, and because of that, it causes many issues.

Simplistically, if ever there is something that you are so comfortable with and so in love with that if God looked at you and said, "Give that away," or "Stop doing that," and your response was "No," then you have a false god that you love more than the only real God. That is dangerous idol worship at its core. People love the world, and we love our possessions, our habits, our addictions, and those become our gods. So technically, I was never truly an atheist, but I was definitely agnostic in regard to the only God that matters because there is only one true God.

That summer, those one hundred or so poems and songs that I had written, most of them were about the craving that I felt for death's warm embrace. They were angry songs, expressing such frustration and resentment toward the girl that lied to me while also expressing that I still loved her. Many lines in those songs are about her lying, about my nightmares, about my wish to die, and finally about me thinking that God abandoned me or never existed. I had many songs that I'd written that were essentially internal existential debates that I had to formulate and put onto paper just to get clarity on my own thought process.

Many were basically poetic cost-and-benefit analyses about life and death to try to make a decision about all of the suicidal temptations that I was brutally battling. They were a more poetic and less famous version of the "To be, or not to be" monologue written by Shakespeare. This is why I recommended in step 8 that you keep some of your writings, so you can go back and see them in the future to see how you've grown and how your writing skill has progressed. It's challenging to relive some of those memories that you may prefer to be forgotten, yet it is also inspiring and encouraging to see your progression over time.

There are many songs that I got rid of and did not save. Typically, these songs were ones that were so dark that I wanted to ensure no one would ever find them. We never know when our time is up, when we will die, so I wanted to make sure those songs would never see the light of day if I happened to kick the bucket. These songs, graphic as they may have been, were necessary to honestly and truly vent about what was in my head.

As time has passed, I've been blessed to look back at all of these tragedies (which I only refer to as tragedies for the sake of this book so that you can understand what I'm talking about) and realize that they were actually blessings. Every single issue in my life has had a positive end result even if it took years to figure out. When I was three years old, I crossed my eyes for too long, and they got stuck; if this didn't happen, I wouldn't be writing this page right now. Let me explain this in some greater detail.

To start, yes, it is possible to cross your eyes until they get stuck. What that caused was a visual impairment known as monocular vision. This is where I can only focus out of one eye at a time with limited control on which eye I'm looking through. This is an interesting condition where, if I straighten my eyes, everything becomes so blurry that I can't read to save my life without corrective lenses. However, if I cross my eyes, I'm able to see slightly more clearly with a headache as a side effect. When I was young, I was naturally athletic and inclined to be a physically driven person. Sports were not really an option for me, though. I'd try to catch a ball, and once that ball was close to my hands, my eyes would switch, and it would actually be a few inches away from where I thought it was, causing the ball to embarrassingly bounce off the side of my hands.

When I was in third grade, my parents put me into gymnastics, a sport that involved no catching and was extremely challenging. To this day, I can still do (almost) all of those things that I learned as a nine-year-old, from flips to bar work. Then from the mats at the gym, I developed warts on my feet. At one point, I had a total of seventy-two warts on my feet, from the ball of my foot to my toes. Many doctors, many creams, many painful months, and I couldn't get rid of them.

Finally, we found these medicated bandages that were the winners. When I turned twelve, my warts were almost gone. My dad was going to coach a youth wrestling team at a local high school, and so I was put onto that team. I was able to compete in that because of the wrestling shoes that prevented the spread of those tiny, little witch bumps. I enjoyed wrestling a lot but developed pink eye from having my face pressed into the mats while wearing contact lenses.

I stopped wearing contacts at that time and stopped wrestling shortly after, though the primary reason for me quitting wrestling was the skintight leotards that I had to wear while getting extremely close to other sweaty dudes...not for me. A year passed, and my feet, after approximately three years, were finally cleared up. My parents told me that once I was in the clear, I could start doing any martial arts that I wanted. After countless hours of research, to the extent that a thirteen-year-old could do, I settled on Brazilian jiujitsu (BJJ).

BJJ was close to wrestling with a few very important differences, the first of which is that you do not have to wear spandex. The second was the practicality of it. The goal of wrestling was to pin your opponent on his back for three seconds to win the match. The goal of BJJ was to get your opponent into a position that would end the fight, period. Instead of holding him in place for three seconds, you choke him out or put him in a joint lock that could prevent him from fighting any further. I started doing BJJ on January 18th of that year, 2009.

About a month passed before another guy who was the same age as me started in class. We were in a youth class for people under sixteen. In the second week of him being in the class, his older sister came to practice one day. I still remember that day. I looked over to the place where parents would sit briefly to see this beautiful girl looking back at me. It turns out that beautiful girl was the sister of the guy that I was fighting. I wasn't sure if she was looking at this cross-eyed weirdo trying to see her clearly or if she was watching her brother fighting the cross-eyed weirdo.

A month later, she joined the class. Though she was sixteen at the time, she was smaller than most of the thirteen-year-olds in the class, and the coaches put her in our class. As time progressed, this guy and I became friends, and two and a half years later, his sister and I started secretly dating. I didn't want him to think I was using him to get to his sister or anything like that, so we were waiting to tell him, though the relationship didn't last long enough for us to reach that point.

Late-night phone calls, constant texting, and fighting each other a few days a week at BJJ was most of what our relationship entailed. She graduated high school that summer while I was beginning my sophomore year the following fall. Eight months after we started our relationship, it ended. During the relationship and even right before it began, I started having dreams that came true. Now I'm not claiming to be psychic or anything stupid like that; rather, I'm just explaining some very odd situations that I still do not understand.

Without adding too much detail, I had a dream that we would get together, and we did. Many dreams occurred in the middle, and every single one that I remembered dreaming came true, like, exactly as I dreamt it. Then at the end of the relationship, I had a dream that she left me. Starting that morning and lasting for seven days, she grew increasingly more distant. On December 23rd of that year, I asked her, "Are you happy?"

Her response was one that made me feel so uneasy and so broken inside. Two days before Christmas, she simply replied, "I don't know." I knew what that meant. An hour of talking passed, and it was over. I was heartbroken and destroyed. She told me that she just needed to be alone for a while to work on herself. That night, it took me hours to fall asleep. While briefly asleep, I dreamt this horrendous nightmare that made the *Saw* movie series look like they were produced by Disney as children's films. I was only asleep for about thirty minutes before waking up, having a severe panic attack.

I rolled out of bed, fell to the floor, and couldn't breathe. I couldn't move, I couldn't yell, I could only feel a devastating case of rubatosis, causing the feeling of a kick drum to beat deeply in my chest. If I didn't know any better, I would have thought I was having a heart attack. I lied on the floor in the fetal position, gasping for air for the next several hours until the sun came up. That dream was the worst thing I had ever seen and definitely the worst thing I have ever imagined. I didn't get any sleep for the next three days after that night.

Finally, after those few days, I fell asleep again only to have the exact same dream, like, exactly the same. Every detail was identical, every action was the same, every word spoken was practically scripted and duplicated flawlessly. This pattern repeated for one and a half years. I dreamt that dream every single time that I slept. Not only was sleep hard for me to achieve, I desperately didn't want to sleep. I didn't want to see the images that my brain was somehow able to conjure. Not long after this, I learned that she had been lying about a couple of things.

One day, due to me being on two hours of sleep for the previous two days, I was training in BJJ and attempted to muscle out of a submission called an Americana. This move has the capability of dislocating your shoulder and fracturing your elbow. I tried to rotate my left arm in the opposite direction but didn't have the energy, and I was too stupid to tap out. Suddenly, I felt an extremely sharp pain deep in my left shoulder as a loud popping sound echoed in my ear, which was followed finally by the sound of my other hand tapping my opponent in rapid succession to give up. I wish I had given up sooner.

A few weeks passed, and I was fighting again with very little sleep, which was now my norm. My opponent got a Kimura on my right arm, which is the exact opposite of an Americana in regard to the direction that it rotates your shoulder. He went to finish it fast and hard, and I was too slow (from lack of energy) to tap out in time, and sure enough—*pop!*

Here I was with a broken heart, mentally damaged mind, torn ligaments in both of my shoulders that had been partially dislocated, and I wasn't done yet. The straw that broke the camel's back or, more accurately, the sweep that broke my back was just that. I was trying to sweep a guy who weighed much more than me. Doing this, my spine twisted severely, every muscle in the right side of my back went into spasm, and my back felt like I was lying on a bed of hot embers.

The pain was extreme, but I didn't want anyone to know. I stopped training and made it home and got up (from almost no sleep) the next day in too much pain to move. A few days passed before my mom took me to a chiropractor. It was the most painful adjustment that I had ever received, even to this day, but it fixed my spine, and I was able to walk again. The pain didn't let up at all, though.

Months passed, and the chiropractor finally recommended that I should go see a specific injury massage therapist. After an hour with her, the pain had finally reduced for the first time in months. This sparked my obsession with anatomy. Meanwhile, I was learning more and more about the lies I'd been told. With every lie that I learned the truth about, with every night that wouldn't bring me rest or peace, with every moment of agonizing physical pain, I turned further and further away from God, thinking that there is no way that a loving God would let this happen.

I finally declared to myself that God isn't real during my few days of being unable to move prior to being slightly fixed. There was no conceivable way that anything could be real if what she had told me wasn't…including God. I even went through a stage where I didn't even think I was real. Put this all together: a mentally unstable, overly emotional, sleep-deprived, brutally injured teenager who had been having the same dream every time he slept for months, who now felt abandoned and alone in a cruel yet nonexistent world by a cruel or nonexistent god. How I didn't kill myself is in and of itself a miracle.

Nevertheless, let's continue. When in high school, during my freshman and sophomore year, I ate lunch alone every day. I only had two friends—one was her brother (who went to a different high school), and the other only ever had one class with me during our last semester of senior year. I was a very lonely kid who was very antisocial and was too nervous and awkward to make new friends. I mention this because this was the first positive that came from this unfortunate series of events. When I was very suicidal, I decided that I didn't care anymore about anything. Granted, I didn't think any-thing was real for a while, but that's beside the point.

I developed one of the most amazing blessings, the ability to not care what people thought of me. Whether it was positive or negative, I didn't care. I started making random jokes in the middle of class, and most of them were dark or edgy, but they made people laugh. This led to me not caring to the point that on my eighteenth birthday, I performed in my first stand-up comedy show. During this, I basically went in front of seventy drunk people and made jokes about having a small penis for five minutes. I didn't care about embarrassing myself, but it made them laugh.

As I mentioned earlier, comedians are often depressed and tell jokes to try to make other people feel happier in their lives, since the comedian can't find happiness in their own lives. The reason I knew this little fun fact is because that is why I started doing stand-up. My run at that was not a long-lived venture, as I eventually gave it up. Nonetheless, it was a direct result of me not caring anymore about the opinions of others.

The second blessing I found from this is my passion for anatomy, which led to an interest in other aspects of human sciences like biology, physiology, sociology, and finally psychology. This obsessive passion gave me additional ways to try to help people and love my neighbors. The job that I have been working for the past several years has been in direct relation to this passion for anatomy as well. Having to memorize every individual muscle in the body and every specificity of it from its origin to its attachment to its function, size, and resilience led me to see that God has blessed me with an amazing ability to recall memories and knowledge that I have learned.

This blessing led to me being able to retain and recall biblical knowledge and church history to the point that I can debate, defend, and teach biblical Christianity very well. Probably what I personally would consider the greatest blessing that God has ever bestowed on me is this ability to remember and share His Word with people.

And finally, at long last, what I would deem to be the most important blessing to come out of this mess, the one that led me to this spot right now, is my complete rejection of God. This was the worst thing that I or anyone could ever do. Yet if I didn't do this, I would never have been able to truly and individually put my full faith and trust in Christ alone for my soul's salvation.

When I found that Bible verse that I mentioned in the prologue, it made me start reading the Bible, but it also made me start down a journey to learn about every major world religion in existence with the purpose of proving them all wrong, including Christianity. Luckily, many people have been able to beat me to this, and I found evidence that proves every belief system wrong, except for biblical Christianity. Historical errors from the Book of Mormon, ridiculous claims that are scientifically unintelligible from Eastern religions like Hinduism and Buddhism, and most importantly, to find that all religions are the same lie about self-righteousness, except for Christianity.

Christianity was the only one I couldn't disprove, so I studied it more in-depth than any other religion to try to disprove it. However, it ended up making me a diehard Christian. Did you know that the Bible presented scientific facts thousands of years before we discovered them? Did you know that in the late 1900s, scientists determined that our sun expanding and burning Earth will be the way Earth will be destroyed? Now did you know that the book of Revelation (written sometime between AD 70 and AD 95) actually has that predicted *(Revelation 16:8)*? Did you know that the OT actually tells us that Earth hangs on nothing *(Job 26:7)*? This wasn't discovered by humans until thousands of years after. Did you know that in 1936 we discovered that Earth's core was liquid? We discovered that it's so hot that Earth's core is literally melted minerals and metals (liquid magma). Again, we discovered this in 1936 scientifically. However, it was already told to us by God through His Word in the Book of Job. According to Henry M. Morris' extensive research, the book of Job is the oldest completed book of the Bible, dating back to approximately 2000 BC. The 28th chapter of Job tells us that Earth's core is liquid. This was about four thousand years before we discovered it!

These are only a few of these, but the list goes on. Entire books have been written on that subject alone, and I'm not trying to reinvent the wheel with this book. From there, I looked into the biblical prophecies and found stuff that still freaks me out about how impossibly accurate the predictions of the Bible turned out to be. There are so many amazing angles to view the Bible in and throughout all of it. The Bible is something that I could *not* disprove at all, not a single verse.

Now on the flip side, I also looked into many individuals who were very anti-Christian, militant atheists and listened to them giving their explanations of why the Bible was wrong. What I found, however, were people who really didn't know the Bible at all. They would cite "contradictions" that are nonexistent when proper context is attributed or when the original language is examined. The only possible contradictions in scripture are due, simply, to translational errors. I often enjoyed looking into these contradictions to see what the translators missed or how the atheistic speaker was just ignorant of context. On accident one day, I ended up finding one that was by far the most difficult contradiction to solve.

I spent about five or six hours in one night reading the same four passages over and over, making comparative charts to mark similarities and differences. There is something that occurs in all four of the synoptic Gospels; it's a scene where a woman is anointing Jesus with oil and people get mad at her *(Matthew 26:6–13, Mark 14:1–9, Luke 7:36–50, John 12:1–11)*. However, there's a difference between Luke's account compared to the others. Many people have tried to justify this with ignorance, saying Luke wasn't there and wrote after the fact. While this is true, it didn't account for the differences.

Let's look briefly at the following similarities:

- A woman is anointing Jesus.
- The event takes place in the house of a man named Simon (which was the most common name at the time, like Brandon, John, or Michael today).
- The woman wipes Jesus's feet with her hair.
- Someone got mad at the woman, and Jesus defended her.

Now to look at the differences below:

- The woman is named to be Mary Magdalene in John's account.
- The woman is unnamed in Matthew, Mark, and Luke.
- The woman is called a sinful woman in Luke.

- Matthew, Mark, and John take place in Bethany in the home of a leper named Simon.
- Luke takes place in the house of a Pharisee whose name is also Simon.
- In Luke, Simon doubts Jesus's divinity because of the woman and gets mad that the sinful woman is touching Him.
- In Matthew, Mark, and John, Judas gets mad at the woman (Mary) for wasting expensive perfume.
- In Luke, Jesus defends her by saying that He forgives her sins and says that she cleaned His feet and poured oil on him while no one else did.
- In Matthew, Mark, and John, Jesus defends the woman (Mary) by saying that she is preparing His body for burial and it's not a waste of the perfume.

With all of these differences, it became confusing until I started comparing deeper and found simply that these are two completely different occasions between Luke and the others. Luke's encounter chronologically happened far earlier into Jesus's ministry than the other accounts. The location is the same in all, except for Luke. Judas gets mad in all, except for Luke. After searching through this and finding my answers, I looked it up to see if anyone else had found this.

I found a YouTube video done by a pastor named Mike Winger, who talked about this subject only two months before I did my research. He arrived at the same conclusions that I did, finding the same incongruencies. Aside from his video, I couldn't find any other explanation on this besides the "Luke was wrong" argument, which is false. So what seemed to be a contradiction in scripture was actually just two separate but similar events, one of which was done to foreshadow the other. This, as I mentioned, took me hours to do, and I got so excited when I finally figured it out. This is the case with all "contradictions" in scripture—they are not actually contradictions when you look into them.

This isn't the case with the Quran or with the Book of Mormon or any other form of religious doctrine. That is one of the reasons why I know that the Bible is correct and all of the others are wrong. This kind of in-depth study has become an obsessive passion of mine, especially in the realm of other variants of Christianity, as well as sects and cults that are based on Christianity but alter the Gospel and are therefore no longer Christians. Recently, over the past five years, Roman Catholicism has been that which I have been diving into at oceanic depths. Many of my friends are Catholics or former Catholics, and I have made it my goal to show them the difference between Romanism and Christianity so that they can make an educated decision for themselves.

The biggest difference is the Gospel. As we have discussed, the biblical Gospel is faith alone in Christ alone. The Gospel, according to the Catholic Church, is faith and works combined. The same as Mormonism, the Jehovah's Witnesses, and many other Christian-based cults. All of these say, "Jesus wasn't good enough, and the Bible was wrong," in their own way. The Catholic Church claims that the Pope is in equal authority to Jesus and that tradition is higher in authority than scripture. Mormonism teaches that Joseph Smith was told by "God and Jesus" (even though Jesus is God and Joseph simply didn't understand the Trinity and, therefore, created a false god based on Christianity) that all the Bibles and religions became corrupted and were wrong. The JWs got their foundation from a newspaper editor named Charles Taze Russell (who didn't like the idea of Hell and didn't understand the Trinity either), who rewrote the Bible to eliminate the concepts of Hell and of the Trinity. His claim was that Jesus is not God, but rather, he was Michael the Archangel, who was the first and greatest creation of Jehovah God, according to their misguided teachings. This is so unbiblical.

So Catholicism still has the correct God and the right concept of the Trinity, but they have the same gospel as these other apostate religions. If you think your works play any part in it, you don't have faith in Christ; rather, you have faith in yourself and in your works. They teach that you must attain your own righteousness, and then

Jesus will cover the rest. The Bible says that Jesus paid the price in full for you and perfected those who believe in him.

> Know that a person is not justified by the works of the law, but by faith in Jesus Christ. So we, too, have put our faith in Christ Jesus that we may be justified by faith in Christ and not by the works of the law, because by the works of the law no one will be justified. *(Galatians 2:16 NIV)*

> I do not set aside the grace of God, for if righteousness could be gained through the law, Christ died for nothing! *(Galatians 2:21 NIV)*

> You who are trying to be justified by the law have been alienated from Christ; you have fallen away from grace. For through the Spirit we eagerly await by faith the righteousness for which we hope. For in Christ Jesus neither circumcision nor uncircumcision has any value. The only thing that counts is faith expressing itself through love. *(Galatians 5:4–6 NIV)*

To circle back briefly to the thoughts and even wishes for death to come over you, I'd like to show you one of the most personal parts of Paul's writing where he, too, contemplated this possibility.

> For I fully expect and hope that I will never be ashamed, but that I will continue to be bold for Christ, as I have been in the past. And I trust that my life will bring honor to Christ, whether I live or die. For to me, living means living for Christ, and dying is even better. But if I live, I can do more fruitful work for Christ. So I really don't know which is better. I'm torn between two desires: I long to go and be with Christ, which

would be far better for me. But for your sakes,
it is better that I continue to live. Knowing this,
I am convinced that I will remain alive so I can
continue to help all of you grow and experience
the joy of your faith. *(Philippians 1:20–25 NLT)*

In finality, I deeply hope that you will take these steps and apply them to your life. I hope that you will be able to not only beat depression but also find true purpose and happiness in your life. I hope that you will live a life worthy of your calling *(Ephesians 4:1)*. Above all of this, I hope and I pray that you will accept the true Gospel and be saved through faith alone in Christ Jesus. Thank you for taking the time and making the effort to better yourself. Thank you for reading. I hope you enjoyed and found useful tips in learning how you can and how I Beat Depression With The Bible.

I have told you these things, so that in me
you may have peace. In this world you will have
trouble. But take heart! I have overcome the
world. *(John 16:33 NIV)*

# Body Language

This chapter I wanted to add as a bonus because it is the only step in this book that is not biblically backed. In fact, it is purely psychological. As I have mentioned, I love psychology and have read countless books on the subject from some of the most renowned psychologists to have ever lived. In combination with this, I have listened to many lectures and an unknown number of interviews, debates, and podcasts surrounding psychology and other similar sciences. One of the things that I have picked up and started to play with the most was body language.

Your body language, essentially, is the majority of the way people communicate. Experts have made the claim that 80 percent of our communication is nonverbal. What this means is, our subconscious brain makes our body do things that we are often not fully aware of. This is our unconscious mind trying to communicate with us and with the world. This is why people will often put themselves into certain positions or do certain soothing gestures when they are uncomfortable, nervous, lying, happy, sad, anxious, excited, fearful, aroused, and every other emotion that one could feel.

Since we do these things without realizing that we are doing them, it can often be difficult for us to pay attention enough to notice in ourselves. Fortunately, that's not the goal. If your subconscious can communicate with the world by positioning your body in specific ways, then why couldn't we reverse-engineer that to instead communicate with our subconscious mind. Instead of letting our brain tell our body to react, we must react in order to rewire our subconscious into thinking differently.

To exemplify this, what do you imagine when you think of a person who is happy? Probably the first thing is a smile. Maybe that their chin is up, their eyes are open, you see crow's feet in the corners of their eyes from smiling so much, they stand up straight, move with confidence, they have this glimmer of hope resting at the forefront of their mind, and it shows through a slight wiggle of their nose or twitches in their nostrils. These people display joy through their nonverbal communicative abilities that are often done by accident. So what if we did these on purpose?

As babies, we do not need to learn that smiling is done when we are happy. We know it instinctually. This is why babies smile when they see their mom or their dad. If you haven't ever seen a video of a visually impaired baby getting glasses and being able to see their mom for the first time, I'd highly recommend looking that up because just the expressive joy on that baby's face could be enough to cure depression for onlookers. It is so precious and so amazing to see. Nonetheless, the point I'm making is that these kids will physically display how happy and overjoyed they are far before they learn how to linguistically articulate these emotions.

If our minds know that smiling means happiness and then we force ourselves to smile sincerely, our brains will start to think that we're happy. This is the idea. Fake it 'til you make it…to the extreme. You are literally going to attempt to brainwash yourself into thinking that you're happy. So what is another thing we do when we are happy? We laugh. I learned long ago that there are two ways to view tragedies in this world: horrific or hilarious. Now this might sound very dark, and I don't mean it to be. When bad things happen, laugh it off. I'm not talking about when someone dies; you'll look like an uncaring sociopath even though this is actually how some people unintentionally display grief. When you get a flat tire, when you stub your toe, when you miss the light because of the moron in the Prius who wouldn't move forward because they are simply too busy hypocritically virtue-signaling to the world: laugh.

Your brain will not become sadistic where it only gets happy from tragic events, but it will start to take disappointment more lightheartedly instead. Soon those little things won't ruin your day so easily, and they will just be another part of life, another obstacle to overcome. With this, we need to begin to think about the problems that you deal with personally. This could be on levels of confidence, happiness, or even personability.

So let's look at confidence and see how one who is insecure about themselves could put off a higher display of self-confidence in order to rewire our brain into thinking that we are confident. Imagine, if you will, someone who is very confident. What are they doing? Let's start at the feet and work our way up. The feet will often be about shoulder-length apart from each other. They will be standing with equal pressure on both feet (they won't be leaning on one leg more than the other with one knee straight and the other slightly bent). The people's feet will often point toward something. If you are talking to someone and you notice, for example, that one or both of their feet begin to point toward an exit, it may be time to end that conversation. On the flip of that, people will tend to point their feet in the direction of someone they like in some capacity. This could be based on attraction, trust, or just someone they are comfortable with or care about.

As an example, after my mother and I were visiting with a friend of mine in the hospital for about an hour, people's feet began telling stories. The friend in the hospital had fractured his femur and wasn't doing much with his feet; my mom, on the other hand, was. After an hour passed, I noticed that not just one but both of her feet started to point toward the door. At this time, I closed the conversation, and we said our goodbyes. She wasn't pointing at the door because she wanted to leave; she was pointing because she had other things that she needed to get done, and those tasks were at the forefront of her mind. So her subconscious brain was telling her body that she needed to leave so she could get other stuff done.

The rule of thumb with this is to notice what your feet are pointing at and how close they are to something. If your feet are close to something, you tend to feel positively toward it. If your feet are trying to stay farther from something yet your body seems to be able to get closer, it shows that you don't feel positive toward it. A good example of this would be standing on a cliff, ledge, or tall building. You will keep your feet far from the edge even though you may bend your body to look over the edge. The same can apply to dog feces on the ground. We will be more inclined to bend down to pick up after our dogs than to squat down with our feet close to it.

Up to the knees of a confident person, their knees will not be locked straight but will be at a full extension to ensure maximum height. In the opposite situation, it is common for a person with negative feelings about themselves to stand with their weight primarily on one leg while letting the other leg relax slightly. You'll notice that you do this quite often throughout the day if you stand a lot, regardless of your mental state. In some cases, it can be from sore or injured feet or legs, but in most cases, this will be done to make yourself feel more comfortable physically and, therefore, more comfortable with yourself mentally. This imbalance in weight distribution will lead to their hips being crooked where it looks like one is higher than the other. The hips of a confident person will be straight, level, and facing their task directly.

If you imagine one's pelvis, you have an almost flat-looking structure with very prominent lateral attributes. If you are speaking to someone who is confident, their hips will be squared off with you. Take both sides of your hips and put an imaginary mark on both of them. Then take the task that you need to accomplish or the person you are speaking with and put another marking in the center of them. Connect all of these markings to create an imaginary triangle where the point is facing the target directly; this is the squared-off position that we are going for.

Going up to the chest, we are going to find some of the most crucial points. If someone is insecure, they will tend to have medially rotated shoulders. Essentially what this means is that they will be slouching where they pull their shoulders forward. This is exactly the opposite of the confident person, who will pull their shoulders back, almost trying to touch their shoulder blades together. Doing this, they will stand up straight, again making them as tall as possible. A bonus with this is that it will correct your posture the more you focus on it and, therefore, will alleviate back pain as well.

When the shoulders are back, the chest will be protruding out even more. For both men and women, this gives off a signal that you are not only confident but also honest and trustworthy. This will make you immediately more approachable. Picture a cartoon villain who is planning on destroying the world. He is going to be hunched forward with his shoulders rounded. He is going to have his shoulders shrugged up to his ears, and he will be rubbing his fingers together as he peers around his own shoulders like a marine who is hugging his cover while doing recon. We want to do the opposite of this.

Someone who is insecure will hold their shoulders very high in a shrugging position as if to try to protect their neck. They are always on defense without knowing it and are therefore going to be guarding their more vulnerable areas. If you were to take a level and place it at their nose, it will always be lower than that imaginary level line. We want it to be equal to that line or above it, almost as if our nose was at a ninety-degree angle to our body. Again, we want to expose our necks to show that we are confident. Tucking our chin will tell others that we are not confident, and we feel that we must protect ourselves emotionally. Someone who hides their neck is typically less approachable than someone who reveals their neck. As a side note, ladies who are hit on too much when you go out in public, try out a turtleneck sweater and see how things change.

The face is going to vary on how confident people will hold their face, so we won't bother with specific expressions. However, we will talk about their eyes. Imagine making eye contact with that cartoon villain; he is going to immediately break eye contact with you and try to keep his shifty eyes darting around. Now imagine making eye contact with a superhero. He will hold eye contact for a moment, maybe even nod his head to acknowledge that he sees you. This is what you must try. If we are avoiding eye contact with people, we will not be displaying confidence but fear instead.

While on the face, we should also talk about the mouth. A confident person will not do a lot with their mouth in specific ways, but a happy person will. A confident person will tend to breathe through their nose most of the time (at least when they aren't physically exerting themselves), keeping their mouth closed unless speaking. In opposition to this, someone who lacks confidence will tend to be what we call a "mouth breather," where they leave their jaw dropped open quite often regardless of what they are doing. Like all of these traits, there can be exceptions, such as an issue with nasal pathways that prevent proper airflow through the nose. As for a happy person, they will smile…a lot. As we discussed earlier in this chapter, we do not learn to smile when happy; we do it instinctively as infants. Our brains make us smile to show that it feels happiness or joy in that moment, so like all of these, smile often to trick your brain.

Looking upward and smiling is something that will instantly start to lift your mood; it's peculiar, but it works. I've seen many articles online about women who are sick of men telling them to smile; while I do think it is a weird thing to tell strangers to smile, the men are onto something. The woman may look unhappy, and the man may be trying to get the woman to trick her brain much like this. He is going at it in a very weird way. Simply telling a joke of some kind could get the woman to smile without sounding creepy. In contradiction to this, you ladies need to be less friendly. Not for a psychological reason; rather, the reason women are often targeted by bad people is that they seem to be friendly and, therefore, weak and easy to victimize. Smiling is wonderful; smiling at strangers…not always a good option.

Dropping down from the face now to the part of the body that we tend to have the best control over—our hands. When you're walking around, put your hands at your side. Of course, cold weather or carrying something will be variables that can affect this but do your best to keep your hands out of your pockets and visible. When talking to people, don't be afraid to talk with your hands; this relaxes the speaker and draws in the attention of the listener. Unless, for whatever reason, you are holding a gun or a knife, then do not talk with your hands! This will have the opposite effect that we desire. To respond to your thoughts, yes, that was a horribly stupid joke, but just enjoy it, anyway!

When you are sitting or standing still, what are your hands doing? Are they touching each other? Are they visible? Where are your thumbs pointing? Are your palms displayed? These may seem very minor, but they express powerfully to people what your subconscious feels. Touching your hands together in front of your body is fine, but just be sure to do it right. The best position to keep your hands in would be what's referred to as the steeple position. This is when you are touching the tips of all of your fingers together.

This is a very good display of confidence. Variations of this would include folding your hands by interlocking your fingers together. Both of these positions put your thumbs facing up, which is good. We want our thumbs, whenever naturally possible, to be pointing upward or at our face. When we do this, we are directing attention to our face, and this is going to be beneficial in meeting with people. It is natural to look at what others are looking at or pointing to. This will actually encourage the other person to keep their eye contact with you longer.

The worst thing we can do is hide our thumbs. Hiding our thumbs says that we are unsure about what we are discussing or about what we are thinking about. We want our thumbs to be up and visible when folding our hands or talking with our hands. Think about when you put your hands in your pockets. Do you put your hands fully into the pocket? Just the thumb? Everything but the thumb? Aside from your hands being cold, if you were to rest with your hands in your front pockets, it's usually just thumbs or everything but thumbs that are going to be in the actual pocket. What this says about you can hold some weight.

Putting just your thumbs in will mean (usually) one of two things. The first would be that you are uncomfortable with or unsure about something, and you are hiding your thumbs as a result. The other option is that you are doing something called framing, which is usually done unconsciously when you are talking to someone you find attractive. This is common to see in people when they are dating. Sometimes people are doing this method of resting for both reasons when on a date. You're shy and nervous, yet you want them to notice you, and that is your brain's way of making your body do something similar to a male peacock exhibiting his feathers to be noticed by a possible mate. This position is done excessively by male models because it frames their genital area and makes the female onlookers find them more attractive subliminally because of the display.

Now for the positioning of the hands where all four fingers are in the pocket while the thumb stays out, this is a very confident way to rest your hands as well. This is putting off an image to people that says you are relaxed and know what's going on. It tells people that if you are asked a question, you will be able to answer them (even if this isn't the case). So when putting your hands in your pockets, try to leave the thumbs out unless you are trying to attract a possible spouse.

Supinating our hands while talking to people is also going to be great. This means rotating your wrist so that your palm is facing up. This is a display that reflects honesty and will also show the listener that you are open to hearing their thoughts on what you are saying. Almost as if you were to receive or offer a gift, your palm would be facing up to hold the gift upon receiving or giving. A fun fact about this is that it is actually harder to lie when your palms are facing up. It will make you feel physically uncomfortable if you aren't being sincere. So this will help you to be more honest in life as well as make others see you as being more trustworthy and approachable.

Where we place our hands is also going to be sending many messages. The suprasternal notch is the little U-shaped bone at the top of your sternum and the base of your throat. When women feel uncomfortable, unsure, offended, defensive, nervous, or scared, it is very common for the woman to cover that suprasternal notch. This is why women will often play with a necklace when they are experiencing these emotions. Many women who are depressed will also do this more often because they tend to feel one or more of these emotions on a very regular basis. So avoid covering this area to trick your brain and onlookers into thinking that you aren't feeling any of the emotions listed.

Crossing your arms is something that is often confused in many ways. It was common to think that this is sending off a message that you are closed off or are defensive, while in reality it's hugging yourself. It's a soothing gesture that is often done when someone is uncomfortable or cold. Though the discomfort could be because of the person being defensive, it is only one possible meaning of this. A good rule of thumb, either way: avoid crossing your arms in public. This, while harmless in meaning, does cause your shoulders to round forward, and it hides your chest. We want our shoulders back and our chest to be visible to the world, as mentioned previously.

Many people, myself included, will feel a need to keep our hands busy and occupied with tasks when in public. An easy way to do this is to have a cell phone in your hand. We want to avoid this as well. As we are doing this, our heads are looking downward; we want our heads up. Our mind is distracted; we want to be aware of our surroundings and pay attention to the world around us. It is okay for your arms to be hanging down at your side in a relaxed way. There is nothing wrong with it despite what your anxious brain tells you. At first, doing this, forcing yourself to hold your arms at your side, will feel very uncomfortable because your mind wants you to do something different. This is often the case for most of these little tricks. Our body puts us into these positions because our mind tells us that they are more comfortable than our current positioning.

As mentioned, our subconscious brain is trying its best to communicate to the world (and to us) about how it's feeling. So it is common for our bodies to seek the comfort that our minds want us to seek. However, when it's seeking to tell us that we are sad, scared, uncomfortable, and many other negative emotions, we must stop it in its tracks and tell it the opposite with our posture and body language. This is how our subconscious brains communicate, so let's speak its language to teach it something. Let's teach it that we are happy physically so that we will start to be happy mentally.

Start paying close attention to the way you move your body and the positions that you place your hands in. Even start to take notes on what your body tends to do the most frequently so you can figure out what to avoid and take care of. For the postural component of pulling your shoulders back, this is common for the chest muscles of a person to be stronger/tighter than their antagonist muscles in the upper back. Due to this, we may need to start working out our upper backs in order to correct this imbalance and make this process easier for us. This can be closely related to step 9 in our efforts to increase our physical health to improve our mental health.

Since this bonus chapter arrived after the conclusion of this book, I felt it would be slightly awkward to just end here suddenly. So I'd like to conclude one final time and encourage you to take all of these steps to heart, take them seriously, and put them into practice in your life. Put Jesus at the center of every thought you have and every action you commit, read the Bible every day, and trust God and God only. I hope that everyone who reads these words will be as successful as I was when I discovered How To Beat Depression With The Bible.

# ABOUT THE AUTHOR

Taylor Johnson has spent an immense amount of time focusing on a single subject: the Bible. Raised in a Christian home, Taylor, like many others, fell far away from the beliefs of his parents when he arrived in his teenage years. Mentally devastating tragedies left Taylor feeling suicidal and depressed, leading him to a complete rejection of God and reality. Taylor set out to disprove religion completely.

Making his way through disproving a few major religions, he then started to read deeply into God's Word in an attempt to disprove Christianity next. After his research concluded that the Bible was without error and was factually proven to be written in a completely impossible way, Taylor became a born-again Christian and was saved by grace alone through faith alone in Christ alone at the age of eighteen.

The Bible calls all believers to repent—this was Taylor's greatest struggle. God blessed Taylor with a new heart and new desires the moment he was saved. However, Taylor's sinful nature was constantly fighting his newly found faith. The figurative angel and demon on his shoulders weren't arguing across his face; they were ripping out each other's still-beating hearts in their battle for Taylor's soul. This only led Taylor's depression to worsen as he feared he could lose God's grace.

When he began reading the Bible daily, studying the original languages, and seeking context, he began to win the battle within himself. He learned the key to life-long repentance and how to resist the temptation to sin: by always keeping Jesus at the forefront of his mind. More importantly, he learned that he could never lose God's grace because salvation is not based on works but by faith alone. Taylor's life's goal became this: to reach the world with God's Word, to use his God-given talent of writing to preach from the pages of a book, to educate those who are lost, and to help guide people back to their creator.

9 7 9 8 8 8 6 1 6 9 6 7 6